Student Team Learning:

A Practical Guide to Cooperative Learning

THIRD EDITION

by Robert E. Slavin

nea PROFESSIONAL LIBRARY
National Education Association
Washington, D.C.

The Author

Robert E. Slavin is Director of the Elementary School Program, Center for Research on Effective Schooling for Disadvantaged Students, The Johns Hopkins University, Baltimore. He is also the author of *Cooperative Learning: Student Teams*, published by NEA.

Printing History
  First Printing: September 1983
  Second Printing: June 1986
  SECOND EDITION: June 1988
  Fourth Printing: October 1989
  THIRD EDITION: October 1991
  Sixth Printing: September 1992

Note

The opinions expressed in this publication should not be construed as representing the policy or position of the National Education Association. Materials published by the NEA Professional Library are intended to be discussion documents for teachers who are concerned with specialized interests of the profession.

Library of Congress Cataloging-in-Publication Data

Slavin, Robert E.
  Student team learning : a practical guide to cooperative learning
by Robert E. Slavin. — 3rd ed.
  p. cm. — (Developments in classroom instruction)
  Includes bibliographical references.
  ISBN 0–8106–1845–1
  1. Group work in education.   2. Team learning approach in
education. I. Title. II. Series.
  LB1032.S546   1991
  371.3'95—dc20   91–24249
                                           CIP

CONTENTS

PART TWO: Student Team/Cooperative Learning: Views and Research

PREFACE TO THE THIRD EDITION

When the first edition of this monograph was published (1983), cooperative learning was in its infancy. Much of the research on the simpler forms was done, but few teachers were making regular use of cooperative methods.

Today, hundreds of thousands of teachers routinely incorporate cooperative learning in their lessons. It is used in all subjects and grade levels from two through college. New methods have been developed and researched; these are described in this edition.

Although the first edition was concerned with introducing the ideas of cooperative learning to teachers who had usually not heard of it, today's concerns have more to do with misconceptions and misuses of cooperative learning. This third edition adds material on current research that emphasizes the importance of group goals and individual accountability as well as material on comprehensive approaches to the three Rs and on tracking and ability grouping. Otherwise, I have maintained the practical down-to earth approach to effective use of cooperative learning presented in the earlier editions. This monograph is adapted from *Using Student Team Learning*, the teacher's manual for the cooperative learning methods developed and researched at Johns Hopkins University.

The research and development that led to Student Team Learning dates back to 1970. Most of the funding for the research has come from the National Institute of Education (NIE) and the Office of Educational Research and Improvement (OERI), U.S. Department of Education, except for research on Student Team Learning and mainstreaming, which was funded by the U.S. Office of Special Education. Development of curriculum materials and dissemination have been supported by NIE, OERI, the National Diffusion Network, and the National Science Foundation.

The methods described in this book are not the work of any single individual. I am primarily responsible for Student Teams-Achievement Divisions (STAD) and, with Marshall Leavey and Nancy Madden, for Team Accelerated Instruction (TAI). Cooperative Integrated Reading and Composition (CIRC) was developed by Nancy Madden, Robert Stevens, and myself. I adapted Jigsaw II from work by Elliot Aronson. Teams-Gates-Tournament is primarily the creation of David DeVries and Keith Edwards. John Hollifield and Gail Fennessey have contributed to the writing of earlier training manuals, of which this book is a descendant. Charles Beady contributed the drawings to this publication.

The opinions expressed in this book are those of the author; they do not represent the policy of the U.S. Department of Education.

Robert E. Slavin

For information concerning any aspect of Student Team Learning, including how to obtain copies of the Teacher's Manual, curriculum materials, filmstrips, regional or local training workshops, the names of state facilitators of the National Diffusion Network, or other information, please contact

The Johns Hopkins Team Learning Project
Center for Social Organization of Schools
Johns Hopkins University
3505 North Charles Street
Baltimore, MD 21218
301-338-8249

PART ONE

Student Team/Cooperative Learning:
How and Why

1. THE METHODS/TECHNIQUES

Do you remember being on a softball team, up at bat, with your teammates behind you shouting, "Hit it a mile!"? You knew you would do your best because your peers depended on you. The thrill of coming through for the team, of being the star even for a day, is one that few people forget. Being on a team, working for a cooperative goal, can be one of the most exciting experiences in life.

Can this kind of peer support for achievement, the easy acceptance of teammates, and the excitement of teamwork be transferred to the classroom? Such authors as James Coleman in *The Adolescent Society* (1961) and Urie Bronfenbrenner in *Two Worlds of Childhood* (1970) have suggested that teams could work in the classroom, and a long tradition of research in social psychology has shown that people working for a cooperative goal come to encourage one another to do their best, to help one another do well, and to like and respect one another (Slavin, 1977a). But how can team learning be made practical and effective in the classroom?

This question touched off 15 years of research and development in classrooms. The result may be one answer to a major contemporary dilemma of schools: techniques that achieve both humanistic educational goals *and* basic skills learning goals instead of achieving one at the expense of the other.

When teachers place students on learning teams, each student knows that a group of peers supports his or her academic efforts. This is true because team success requires that all members do their best. Think back to the softball game. If you got that hit, your teammates went wild with approval; if you didn't, they consoled you and began encouraging the next batter. Can you remember anything like that happening in class? If you can, it was probably in a team spelling bee or other team activity in which your academic efforts could help a group achieve success.

Educational research has demonstrated that heterogeneous teams made up of high and low achievers, boys and girls, Blacks, whites, and Hispanics, can be successfully transplanted from the playing field to the classroom. Several Student Team Learning techniques have now been extensively researched and found to significantly increase student learning. Some are designed for specific subjects and grade levels, and some are generic, broadly applicable methods. The latter, which are emphasized in this book, include Student Teams-Achievement Divisions (STAD), Teams-Games-Tournament (TGT), and Jigsaw.

STUDENT TEAMS-ACHIEVEMENT DIVISIONS

In STAD, the simplest of the Student Team Learning methods, students are assigned to four- or five-member learning teams. Each team is a microcosm of the entire class, made up of high-, average-, and low-performing students; boys and girls; and students of different racial or ethnic backgrounds. Each week, the teacher introduces new material in a lecture or a discussion. Team members then study worksheets on the material. They may work problems one at a time in pairs, take turns quizzing each other, discuss problems as a group, or use whatever means they wish to master the material. The students also receive worksheet answer sheets making clear to them that their task is to learn the concepts, not simply to fill out the worksheets. Team members are told they have not finished studying until all are sure they understand the material.

Following team practice, students take quizzes on the material they have been studying. Teammates may *not* help one another on the quizzes; they are on their own. The quizzes are scored in class or soon after; then the individual scores are formed into team scores by the teacher.

The amount each student contributes to his or her team is determined by the amount the student's quiz score exceeds his or her past quiz average. This improvement score system gives every student a good chance to contribute maximum points to the team if (and only if) the student does his or her best, showing substantial improvement or completing a perfect paper. Use of improvement scores has been shown to increase student academic performance even without teams (Slavin 1980), but it is especially important as a component of Student Team Learning. Think back to the baseball game; the one problem in that sport is the automatic strikeout, the team member who cannot hit the ball no matter how much he or she practices. In Student Team Learning, no one is an automatic strikeout; and by the same token, no one is guaranteed success because it is improvement that counts.

A weekly one-page class newsletter recognizes the teams with the highest scores. The newsletter also recognizes the students who exceeded their own past records by the largest amounts or who completed perfect papers.

Student Teams-Achievement Divisions are not difficult to use. Following the steps outlined in this book, teachers need only assign their students to teams, allow team members to study together, give regular quizzes, and do 30 to 40 minutes of team scoring at the end of the week. However, the change in the classroom is dramatic. Suddenly, students begin helping each other learn basic skills instead of resenting those who know the answers and making fun of those who do not. They begin to see the teacher as a resource person who has valuable information that they need to accomplish something important, more like a coach than a boss. They begin to see learning activities as social instead of isolated, fun instead of boring, under their own control instead of the teacher's. They begin to feel a camaraderie toward their classmates that is common on the athletic field but not in the classroom. In the integrated classroom, this new sense of camaraderie extends across racial or ethnic barriers to create new friendships less likely to exist in the traditional classroom. In the mainstreamed classroom, this camaraderie extends across an even larger barrier, that between physically or mentally handicapped students and their classmates, to create a climate of acceptance instead of scapegoating. Researchers have documented all these effects of Student Team Learning and many others (see Chapter 2 on research evidence); what is so striking is that all these outcomes stem from the same simple change in classroom procedure.

TEAMS-GAMES-TOURNAMENT

Teams-Games-Tournament uses the same teams, instructional format, and worksheets as STAD. In TGT, however, students play academic games to show their individual mastery of the subject matter. Students play these games in weekly tournaments in which they compete with members of other teams who are comparable in past performance. The competitions take place at tournament tables of three students. Thus, a high-performing student from the Fantastic Four might compete with a high performer from the Pirates and a high performer from the Superstars. Another table might have average-performing students from the Pirates, the Masterminds and the Chiefs; and yet another might have low performers from the Superstars, the Tigers, and the Masterminds. Of course, the students are not told which is the highest table, which is next, and so on, but they are told that their competition will always be fair. Although teams stay together for about six weeks, the tournament table assignments change every week according to a system that maintains the equality of the competition. Equal competition makes it possible for students of all levels of past performance to contribute maximum points to their teams if they do their best, in the same way that the improvement score system in STAD makes it possible for everyone to be successful.

After the tournament, team scores are figured and a newsletter recognizes the highest-scoring teams and tournament table winners. Thus TGT uses the same pattern of teaching, team worksheet study, individual assessment, equal opportunities for success, and team recognition as that used in Student Teams-Achievement Divisions, but the use of academic games instead of quizzes makes TGT even more exciting and motivating than STAD. In fact, Teams-Games-Tournament generates so much excitement that getting students to stop can be a problem. For example, in one study in a Baltimore junior high school attended by a substantial number of students bused from the inner city, all the students in two classes stayed after school (and missed their buses) to attend a tie-breaker playoff in a tournament. Teachers using Teams-Games-Tournament have reported that students never particularly interested in school were coming after class for materials to take home to study, asking for special help, and becoming active in class discussions.

JIGSAW

STAD and TGT were developed at Johns Hopkins University. Jigsaw, however, was originally designed by Elliot Aronson and his colleagues at the University of Texas and then at the University of California at Santa Cruz. In the Jigsaw method, students are assigned to six-member teams; academic material is broken down into five sections. For example, a biography may be divided into early life, first accomplishments, family life, major setbacks, and later life. First, each team member reads his or her unique section. If no students are absent, two students share a section. Next, members of different teams who have studied the same sections meet in "expert groups" to discuss their sections. Then students return to their teams and take turns teaching their teammates about their sections. Since the only way students can learn about sections other than their own is to listen carefully to their teammates, they are motivated to support and show interest in each other's work.

This book emphasizes Jigsaw II, a modification of Jigsaw developed at Johns Hopkins University. In Jigsaw II, students work in four- to five-member teams, as in Teams-Games-Tournament and Student Teams-Achievement Divisions. Instead of each student having a unique section, all students read a common narrative, such as a book chapter, a short story, or a biography. However, each student receives a topic on which to become an expert. Students with the same topics meet in expert groups to discuss them, and return to their teams to teach their teammates what they have learned. Then students take individual quizzes, which are formed into team scores using the improvement score system of STAD, and a class newsletter recognizes the highest-scoring teams and individuals. Jigsaw II is easier to use than original Jigsaw because the teacher need not write separate readings for each topic.

For more information on the original Jigsaw method, see *The Jigsaw Classroom* (Aronson et al. 1978).

TEAM ACCELERATED INSTRUCTION

Team Accelerated Instruction (TAI) is a combination of individualized instruction and team learning designed for use in elementary and middle school mathematics classes. In TAI, students work in the same heterogeneous teams as in the Student Team Learning methods (STAD, TGT, and Jigsaw II). However, whereas in Student Team Learning all students study the same materials at the same rate, in TAI, students are placed in individualized mathematics materials anywhere from addition to algebra, according to a placement test, and then work at their own levels and rates. Teammates check each other's work against answer sheets, except for final tests, which are scored by student monitors (who change each day). Team scores are based on the average number of units completed each week by the team members and the accuracy of the units; teams that meet a present criterion receive attractive certificates or other rewards. The teams and the monitors manage all the routine checking, assignment, and materials-handling parts of the individualized program, freeing the teacher to work with individuals and homogeneous math groups. Because it is an individualized program, TAI is especially appropriate for use in heterogeneous math classes—such as those containing mainstreamed, low-achieving students and/or gifted students.

COOPERATIVE INTEGRATED READING AND COMPOSITION

The newest of the Student Team Learning methods is a comprehensive program for teaching reading and writing in the upper elementary grades (Stevens et al. 1987). In Cooperative Integrated Reading and Composition (CIRC), teachers use basal readers and reading groups, much as in traditional reading programs. However, students are assigned to teams composed of pairs of students from two different reading groups. While the teacher is working with one reading group, students in the other groups are working in their pairs on a series of cognitively engaging activities, including reading to one another, making predictions about how narrative stories will come out, summarizing stories to one another, writing responses to stories, and practicing spelling, decoding, and vocabulary. Students work in teams to master main idea and other comprehension skills. During language arts periods, students engage in writing drafts, revising and editing one another's work, and preparing team or class books for publication.

SIMILARITIES AND DIFFERENCES AMONG METHODS

Student Teams-Achievement Divisions, Teams-Games-Tournament, and Jigsaw II share several features:

1. Four- to five-member, heterogeneous learning teams
2. Reward-for-improvement scoring (or equal competition)
3. Team recognition.

The weekly sequence of activities in these methods, however, is not the same. Figure 1 outlines the basic schedule for each method.

The difference between STAD and TGT comes after students have studied in their teams. In STAD, students take a quiz to show how much they have learned, and their team scores are based on the amount each team member has gained in achievement over his or her past record. In TGT, after the teaching and team study components, instead of taking a quiz students compete at ability-homogenous tournament tables against representatives of other teams to show how much they have learned, and team scores are based on the team members' tournament points.

In Jigsaw II, the initial information input is from textual materials instead of (or in addition to) teacher instruction. Each team member receives an expert topic. After reading, students discuss their topics in expert groups composed of all other students in the class who have the same topic. After the discussion, students report to their teams. Then everyone is quizzed, and improvement points and team scores are computed as in STAD.

2. THE RESEARCH EVIDENCE

POSITIVE OUTCOMES

Research provides evidence of positive outcomes from student teams/cooperative learning in many areas, including student achievement, integration, mainstreaming, and self-esteem.

Student Achievement

For a teacher deciding whether or not to use a new instructional method, the first question is usually, "Will it increase my students' learning?"

In the case of Student Team Learning, the answer is "Yes, in most cases." Teachers can feel confident that if they use these methods as described in this book, students will learn at least as well as and probably better than they will with traditional methods.

Forty studies of at least four weeks' duration have evaluated Student Teams-Achievement Divisions, Teams-Games-Tournament, Team Accelerated Instruction, and Cooperative Integrated Reading and Composition. In all the studies, which took place in regular classrooms without aides or special resources, one of the Student Team Learning methods was compared to traditionally taught classes studying the same material. In 33 of the 40 studies, the students in the Student Team Learning classes learned significantly more than those in the traditionally taught classes; in 7, there were no differences (Slavin 1987c). In most of these studies, teachers or classes were randomly assigned to Student Team Learning or traditional methods, the treatments were used for at least six weeks, and care was taken to ensure that the traditionally taught classes had the same curriculum materials as the Student Team Learning classes. Such a high success rate in well-controlled studies is unusual in research on new instructional methods.

Student Teams-Achievement Divisions. STAD have been evaluated in 21 studies involving students in grades two through ten, in schools from inner-city Baltimore and Philadelphia to suburban Maryland, rural Maryland and Georgia to Nigeria, Israel, and West Germany. The subject areas have included language arts, mathematics, reading, science, and social studies. In 16 of the studies, STAD were found to increase learning more significantly than traditional methods; in five there were no differences (Slavin 1978). STAD have been approved by the Joint Dissemination Review Panel (JDRP), a U.S. Department of Education agency that examines research evidence on new programs and certifies for dissemination those that meet stringent requirements.

Teams-Games-Tournament. TGT has been evaluated in 9 studies in regular classrooms involving nearly 3,000 students in grades 3 to 12. Like STAD, TGT has been studied in all kinds of schools in different parts of the

Figure 1: **Basic Schedule of Activities for STAD, TGT, and Jigsaw II**

Student Teams-Achievement Divisions	Teams-Games-Tournament	Jigsaw II
TEACH	**TEACH**	**TEXT**
TEAM STUDY	**TEAM STUDY**	**TALK**
TEST	**TOURNAMENT**	**TEAM REPORT**
		TEST
TEAM RECOGNITION	**TEAM RECOGNITION**	**TEAM RECOGNITION**

United States. These studies have involved mathematics, language arts, social studies, and reading (Slavin 1977c). In eight of the studies, TGT students learned significantly more than traditionally taught students; in the ninth, there were no differences. Based on this research evidence, TGT has been approved for dissemination by the JDRP.

Team Accelerated Instruction. Some of the largest effects of Student Team Learning methods have been found in studies of TAI. Five of six studies found substantially greater learning of mathematics computations in TAI than in control classes; one study found no differences (Slavin 1985c). Across all six studies, the TAI classes gained an average of twice as many grade equivalents on standardized mathematics computations measures as traditionally taught control classes. For example, in one 18-week study in Wilmington, Delaware, the control group gained .61 grade equivalents in mathematics computations while the TAI classes gained 1.65 grade equivalents (Slavin and Karweit 1985). These experimental-control differences were still substantial (though smaller) a year after the students were in TAI. TAI has also been approved for dissemination by the JDRP.

Cooperative Integrated Reading and Composition. Two studies of CIRC (Stevens et al. 1987) found substantial positive effects of this method on standardized tests of reading comprehension, reading vocabulary, language expression, language mechanics, and spelling in comparison to traditional control groups. The CIRC classes gained 30 to 70 percent of a grade equivalent more than control classes on these same measures in both studies. In addition, positive effects of CIRC were found on writing and on oral reading skills.

Integration

One of the most important effects of Student Team Learning is on friendships among students of different ethnic backgrounds in desegregated classes. Anyone who has spent much time in a desegregated secondary school knows that white students associate mostly with white students, Blacks with Blacks, Hispanics with Hispanics, and so on. This situation is always disappointing to those who hoped that widespread desegregation would led to greatly increased contact, and thereby respect and liking, among students of different ethnic backgrounds. It should perhaps not be too surprising, however, because in most desegregated schools Black, white, and Hispanic students come from separate neighborhoods, ride different buses, and often attended different elementary schools.

In several studies that did not use Student Team Learning, students in traditionally structured, racially mixed classes were asked to name their friends (Gerard and Miller 1975). When the question was repeated a semester later, the proportion of Black students who named whites as their friends and whites who named Blacks either stayed the same or decreased. Apparently, assigning Black and white students to the same classes does not by itself increase friendship across racial lines.

A team solution. Student Team Learning is an obvious solution to the problem of integrating the desegregated classroom. We know from decades of research that when people work together for a common goal, they gain in respect and liking for one another. When Student Team Learning techniques were applied in Desegregated classrooms, that was the finding. In three studies, the number of friends of a different ethnic group named by TGT students increased far more than did those of control students (DeVries, Edwards, and Slavin 1978). Three additional studies found STAD to have the same effect (Slavin 1977b, 1979; Slavin and Dickle 1981). In fact, in many of these studies, the Student Team Learning students began to choose their classmates as friends as if ethnicity were no barrier to friendship. This never happened in the control classes. Jigsaw II has also been found to improve relationships across ethnic group lines (Gonzales 1979; Ziegler 1981). In one of the STAD studies, the positive effects on intergroup relations were found to be present nine months after the end of the study (Slavin 1979). Traditionally taught students named few students outside their own racial groups as friends on the followup questionnaire, but former STAD students had many friends of a different race. A Toronto study also found positive effects of Jigsaw II on cross-ethnic friendships five months after the conclusion of the study (Ziegler 1981). The Joint Dissemination Review Panel has approved Student Team Learning as a whole (STAD, TGT, and Jigsaw II) for dissemination because of the effects of these methods on intergroup relations.

Mainstreaming

Although ethnicity is a major barrier to friendship, it is not as large as the barrier between physically or mentally handicapped children and their normal-progress peers. The mandate of Public Law 94-142 to place as many children as possible in regular classrooms has created an unprecedented opportunity for handicapped children to take their place in the mainstream of society. But it has also created enormous practical problems for classroom teachers and has often led to social rejection of the handicapped children.

Once again, Student Team Learning is an answer. In the Student Team Learning classroom, mainstreamed students are assigned to teams just as other students are. If these students are physically handicapped, their classmates come to value the contribution they make to the team, but more importantly they come to see them as important individuals, not just as handicapped persons. If the mainstreamed students are academically handicapped, their opportunity to contribute points to their teams for showing improvement (STAD and Jigsaw) or for succeeding in competition with others of similar performance levels (TGT) also makes these students valued by their teammates. The teamwork makes them part of the group, instead of separate and different, and provides them with teammates who encourage and assist their academic progress.

The research on Student Team Learning and mainstreaming has focused on the academically handicapped student. One study used STAD to attempt to integrate students performing two years or more below the level of their peers into the social structure of the classroom. The use of STAD significantly reduced the degree to which the normal-progress students rejected their mainstreamed classmates and increased academic achievement and self-esteem of all students, mainstreamed as well as normal-progress (Madden and Slavin 1983a). Research on Team Accelerated Instruction has also found positive effects on the acceptance of mainstreamed students as well as on the achievement, self-esteem, and positive behavior of all students (Slavin, Leavy, and Madden 1982). TAI combines individualized instruction with team learning in mathematics, offering students the academic benefits of material at their own level and the academic and social benefits of working in cooperating teams. Other research using cooperative teams has also shown significant improvements in relationships between mainstreamed academically handicapped students and their normal-progress peers (Ballard et al. 1977; Cooper et al. 1980).

Perhaps the most important fact about Student Team Learning in classes containing mainstreamed students is that these techniques are good not only for these children, but also for all children. Student Team Learning offers the teacher a chance to incorporate the mainstreamed children into the classroom social system and meet their individual needs while allowing the teacher to do even better with and for their normal-progress peers.

Self-Esteem

One of the most important aspects of a child's personality is self-esteem. Many people have assumed that self-esteem is a relatively stable personal attribute that schools have little ability to change. However, several researchers working on Student Team Learning techniques have found that teams do increase students' self-esteem. Students in Student Team Learning and TAI classes have been found to feel better about themselves than do students in traditional classes. These improvements in self-esteem have been found for TGT (DeVries, Lucasse, and Shackman 1979), for STAD (Madden and Slavin 1983a), for Jigsaw (Blaney et al. 1977), for the three methods combined (Slavin and Karweit 1981), and for TAI (Slavin, Leavey, and Madden 1982).

Why does this occur? First, it has been consistently found that TGT and STAD students report that they like others and feel liked by others more than control students do (Slavin 1987c). Liking of others and feeling liked by others are obvious components of feeling worthwhile. Second, it seems likely that students feel (and are) more successful in their school work when they work in teams. This could also lead to an increase in self-esteem. Whatever the reason, the effect of Student Team Learning on self-esteem may be particularly important for long-term effects on mental health.

Other Outcomes

In addition to student achievement, positive race relations, mainstreaming, and self-esteem, effects of Student Team Learning have been found on a variety of other important educational outcomes. Increased positive interaction among emotionally disturbed adolescents has been found in two studies of TGT (Slavin 1977c; Janke 1988). Other positive effects include liking of school, peer norms in favor of doing well academically, student feelings of control over their own fate in school, and student cooperativeness and altruism (Slavin 1983a). TGT (DeVries and Slavin 1978) and STAD (Slavin 1978) have been found to have positive effects on students' time on task, a variable that is coming to take on increased importance as educators become more concerned about instructional effectiveness. TAI has been found to improve students' classroom behavior, friendships behaviors, and self-confidence (Slavin, Leavey, and Madden 1982). The striking feature of this research is the breadth of outcomes associated with the various team learning methods. One method may improve student achievement, another race relations, a third student self-esteem. But how many educational methods can claim to have documented so many different effects in well-controlled field experiments in schools? Positive effects on all variables measured are not found in every Student Team Learning study, but negative effects are almost never found and the ratio of significantly positive to equal findings on the major variables (achievement, race relations, self-esteem) is about three to one (Slavin 1983a, 1987c).

IS STUDENT TEAM LEARNING PRACTICAL?

Many educational innovations introduced in recent years have required enormous amounts of teacher training and/or money to implement. Fortunately, Student Team Learning techniques are quite simple. Thousands of teachers located in every state have used Teams-Games-Tournament, Student Teams-Achievement Divisions, or Jigsaw with nothing more than a one-day workshop, a teacher's manual similar to this book, and available curriculum materials. Many have used these methods with the manual alone. Teachers can obtain curriculum materials for TGT, STAD, and CIRC in most elementary and secondary subjects, distributed at cost by the Johns Hopkins Team Learning Project (3505 North Charles Street, Baltimore, MD 21218), or they can make their own materials. TAI-Mathematics is distributed by Mastery Education Corporation (85 Main Street, Watertown, MA 02172). Student Team Learning methods have been used in grades one through college (although mostly in grades two through twelve), in subjects ranging from math to science to social studies to English to foreign language, in every part of the United States and in several foreign countries. They have been used for purposes ranging from improving basic skills for average students to bringing low-performing students up to grade level and to providing a richer experience for gifted students. They have often been used specifically to improve race relations, to make mainstreaming more effective, or just to help students become more excited about school. Not every teacher will feel comfortable using Student Team Learning, but most who do are enthusiastic, and many report dramatic differences in their own feelings about teaching.

As noted earlier, STAD, TGT, and TAI are certified by the U.S. Department of Education's Joint Dissemination Review Panel for their effects on basic skills, and the entire Student Team Learning program is certified by the JDRP for effects on intergroup relations. This means that these programs are eligible for dissemination by the National Diffusion Network, which has a system of state facilitators in every state who help school districts adopt JDRP-approved programs.

3. A PRACTICAL GUIDE

Which method should you use? No single instructional method can be used in all subject areas and for all purposes equally well; Student Team Learning is no exception. However, there are different methods based on cooperative, heterogeneous teams for almost all instructional circumstances. Student Teams-Achievement Divisions and Teams-Games-Tournament can be used to teach any material in which questions with one right answer can be posed. This includes most material taught in mathematics, language arts, science, foreign language, and some parts of social studies, such as geography, graph or map skills, and any knowledge-level objectives. Jigsaw II is used most often in social studies, but it can also be applied to literature or parts of science in which students learn from narrative materials. Team Accelerated Instruction is restricted to mathematics in grades two through eight; it is most needed in heterogeneous math classes, where all students should not be taught the same materials at the same rate. Cooperative Integrated Reading and Composition is restricted to reading, writing, and language arts instruction in grades two through six. Besides subject matter, there are other reasons teachers may choose one Student Team Learning method over another. Figure 2 summarizes the advantages and most appropriate subjects for STAD, TGT, Jigsaw II, TAI, and CIRC. Before deciding on a method, it will be helpful to read the descriptions of each method that follow.

STUDENT TEAMS-ACHIEVEMENT DIVISIONS

STAD are made up of five major components: class presentations, teams, quizzes, individual improvement scores, and team recognition.

1. **Class presentations.** The teacher initially introduces the material in a class presentation. In most cases, this is a lecture/discussion, but it can include an audiovisual presentation. Class presentations in Student Teams-Achievement Divisions differ from usual teaching only in that they must clearly focus on the STAD unit. Thus students realize that they must pay careful attention during the presentation because doing so will help them do well on the quizzes, and their quiz scores determine their team scores.

2. **Teams.** Teams are composed of four or five students who represent a cross-section of the class in academic performance, sex, and race or ethnicity. The major function of the team is to prepare its members to do well on the quizzes. After the teacher presents the material, the team meets to study worksheets or

other material. The worksheets may be obtained from the Johns Hopkins Team Learning Project (see the preface for the address), or they may be teacher-made materials (see Chapter 4, Appendix C). Most often, the study takes the form of students quizzing one another to be sure that they understand the content, or of students working problems together and correcting any misconceptions that may have caused teammates to make mistakes.

The team is the most important feature of STAD. At every point, the emphases are on the members doing their best for the team and on the team doing its best for the members. The team provides important peer support for academic performance; it also provides the mutual concern and respect that are important for producing such outcomes as improved intergroup relations, self-esteem, and acceptance of mainstreamed students.

3. **Quizzes.** After one to two periods of teacher presentation and one to two periods of team practice, students take individual quizzes composed of course-content-relevant questions. The quizzes are designed to test the knowledge the students have gained from class presentations and team practice. During the quizzes students are not permitted to help one another. This ensures that every student is individually responsible for knowing the material.

4. **Individual improvement scores.** The idea behind the individual improvement scores is to give each student a performance goal that he or she can reach, but only by working harder than in the past. Any student can contribute maximum points to his or her team in this scoring system, but no student can do so without showing definite improvement over past performance. Each student is given a "base" score, the minimum score to achieve on each quiz. Then students earn points for their teams based on the amount their quiz scores exceed their base scores. After every two quizzes, base scores are recomputed—to challenge students who start performing better to improve further and to adjust to a more realistic level the base scores that were set too high for other students.

5. **Team recognition.** A newsletter is the primary means of rewarding teams and individual students for their performance. Each week the teacher prepares a newsletter to announce team scores. The newsletter also recognizes individuals showing the greatest improvement or completing perfect papers and reports cumulative team standings. In addition to or instead of the newsletter, many teachers use bulletin boards, special privileges, small prizes, or other rewards to emphasize the idea that doing well as a team is important.

Figure 2: User's Guide to Student Team Learning Methods

STAD

Use in grades 2–12 in
- Mathematics
- Language arts
- Science
- Social studies skills, such as geography, graph reading
- Foreign language
- Any material with single right answers.

Advantages:
- Frequent quizzes give feedback to students and teacher.
- Relatively quiet, businesslike form of Student Team Learning.
- Improvement scores challenge students.
- Takes less instructional time than TGT.
- Curriculum materials available in most subjects.

TGT

Use in grades 2–12 in
- Mathematics
- Language arts
- Science
- Social studies skills, such as geography, graph reading
- Foreign language
- Any material with single right answers.

Advantages:
- Student enjoy tournaments.
- Fair competion challenges students.
- Students do most scoring.
- Curriculum materials available in most subjects.

Jigsaw II

Use in grades 3–12 in
- Social studies, when students are learning from books or other readings
- Literature
- Science
- Any material when information comes from books or other readings.

Advantages:
- Can be used for more open-ended objectives.
- Students take real responsibility for teaching teammates.
- Students exercise reading, teaching, discussing, and listening skills.
- Frequent quizzes give feed-back to students and teacher.
- Improvement scores challenge students.
- Easily adapted to library research projects.

TAI

Use in grades 2–8 in
- Mathematics

Advantages:
- Individualization provides for needs of all students, gives students success at their own level.
- Students do almost all scoring and manage materials.
- Materials are completely pre-pared; very little out-of-class time needed.
- Materials cover skills from addition to algebra.
- Students usually learn math skills rapidly.

CIRC

Use in grades 2–6 in
- Reading
- Writing
- Language arts.

Advantages:
- Combination of mixed-ability teams and same-ability reading groups allows students to succeed at their own levels.
- Reading program replaces work-books with engaging activities supported by reading research.
- Writing program provides practi-cal approach to the writing pro-cess that combines writing and language arts instruction.

STAD may be used for part of the instruction, with other methods used for other parts. For example, many English teachers use STAD three periods each week to teach language mechanics and usage, but they teach literature and writing in the two remaining periods using other methods. STAD may also be used in combination with TGT or Jigsaw II.

Getting Ready for Student Teams-Achievement Divisions

Prepare Materials

STAD can be used either with curriculum materials specifically designed for Student Team Learning and distributed by the Johns Hopkins Team Learning Project (see the preface for the address) or with teacher-made materials (see Chapter 4, Appendix C for instructions). Currently, Johns Hopkins materials are available in grade two through eight mathematics; high school consumer mathematics, algebra I, and geometry; elementary and junior high school language arts; elementary and secondary school nutrition; and junior high school life science, physical science, and U.S. history.

For each unit, which should take from three to five days of instruction, a worksheet, a worksheet answer sheet, a game, and a game answer sheet are needed.

Assign Students to Teams

A Student Teams-Achievement Divisions team consists of four or five students who represent a cross-section of the class in terms of sex, race or ethnicity, and past performance. Thus, in a class that is one-half male, one-half female, three-quarters white, and one-quarter minority, a four-person team should include two boys and two girls, of which three are white and one is minority. The team should also include one high performer, one low performer, and two average performers. Of course, "high" and "low" are relative terms, relating to high and low for the class rather than to high or low compared to national norms.

It is the teacher who should assign students to teams, taking into account student likes, dislikes, and "deadly combinations" as well as criteria for a representative class cross-section. The following steps should be used:

Step 1: **Copy Team Summary and Game Score Sheets from Appendix E (in Chapter 4).** Before assigning students to teams, make one copy of a Team Summary Sheet for every four students in the class and one copy of a Game Score Sheet for every team for every three weeks that TGT will be used.

Step 2: **Rank students.** On a sheet of paper, rank students in the class from highest to lowest in terms of past performance. Use whatever information is available: test scores, grades, teacher judgment. If exact ranking is difficult, do the best you can.

Step 3: **Decide on the number of teams.** Each team should have four members if possible. Divide the number of students in the class by four. If the division is even, the quotient will be the number of teams to have. For example, a class of 32 students will have eight four-member teams. If the division is uneven, the remainder will be one, two, or three, so that there may be one, two, or three teams composed of five members. For example, a class of 30 students will have seven teams—five with four members and two with five members.

Step 4: **Assign students to teams.** First, balance the teams according to *performance:* Each team should be composed of students whose performance levels range from low to average to high; and the average performance level of all teams in the class should be approximately equal. Thus students with different performance levels will be able to tutor each other; and no single team will have an advantage in terms of academic performance.

Use the list of students ranked by performance made in Step 2 and assign team letters to each student. For example, in an eight-team class, use the eight letters A through H, as in Figure 3, starting at the top with the letter A. After using the last team letter, continue lettering but in the opposite order. In Figure 3, the students ranked eighth, ninth, twenty-sixth, and twenty-seventh comprise the H team; the students ranked first, sixteenth, nineteenth, and thirty-fourth go on the A team. Note that the students ranked seventeenth and eighteenth are not yet assigned. They will be assigned to teams as fifth members.

Now check the teams for sex and race or ethnicity balance. For example, when one-fourth of a class is Black, approximately one student on each team should be Black; and when a class has more than two major ethnic groups, their proportions should be reflected in team membership. If teams balanced by performance are not balanced by race or ethnicity and sex—and they rarely are on the first try—trade students of the same approximate performance level among teams and place fifth members as available and needed until there is a balance.

Step 5: **Fill in the names of the students on Team Summary Sheets,** leaving the team name blank, after assigning all students to teams. If there are six or more teams, divide them into two leagues. (Many teachers name the two leagues—e.g., American and National.)

Figure 3: Assigning Students to Teams

	Rank Order	Team Name
High-Performing Students	1	A
	2	B
	3	C
	4	D
	5	E
	6	F
	7	G
	8	H
Average-Performing Students	9	H
	10	G
	11	F
	12	E
	13	D
	14	C
	15	B
	16	A
	17	
	18	
	19	A
	20	B
	21	C
	22	D
	23	E
	24	F
	25	G
	26	H
Low-Performing Students	27	H
	28	G
	29	F
	30	E
	31	D
	32	C
	33	B
	34	A

Determine Initial Base Scores

In addition to assigning students to teams, it is necessary to determine the initial base score for each student. A base score is the minimum the teacher expects the student to make on a 30-item quiz. Refer to the ranked list of students made in assigning students to teams in Step 2. If the class has 25 or more students, give the first three students an initial base score of 20; the next three, 19; the next three, 18; and so on until you have assigned each student an initial base score. Put the base scores on a Quiz Score Sheet (see Chapter 4, Appendix E). If the class has 24 or fewer students, give the first two students an initial base score of 20; the next two, 19; and so on. Note that these base scores are just a start; they will be modified to reflect students' actual scores after every two quizzes. When these adjustments are made, the base score will eventually be set approximately 5 points below the student's average past quiz scores. If there are students at the very bottom of the list that the teacher feels have little chance of making even their base scores, their base scores should be set a little lower according to teacher judgment. Don't worry about setting base scores exactly; they will adjust themselves over time.

Activities

As shown in Figure 1, Student Teams-Achievement Divisions consist of regular cycles of instructional activities: teach, team study, test, and team recognition.

TEACH

Time: One to two class periods
Main Idea: **Present the lesson**
Materials Needed: Lesson plan

Each lesson in TGT begins with a class presentation. A filmstrip or movie or other technique can be used to introduce the lesson, but most teachers simply give a lecture/discussion. In the lesson, stress the following (adapted from Good and Grouws 1979):

- *Briefly review* any prerequisite skills or information.
- Stick close to the *objectives* that you will test.
- Focus on *meaning,* not memorization.
- Actively *demonstrate* concepts or skills, using visual aids and many examples.
- Frequently *assess* student comprehension by asking many questions.
- Have all students *work problems* or *prepare* answers to your questions.
- Call on students *at random* so that they will never know who is going to have to answer a question. This makes all students prepare themselves to answer. *Do not* just call on students who raise their hands.

- *Do not give long class assignments* at this point. For example, have students work one or two problems or prepare one or two answers and then give them feedback.
- Always *explain* why an answer is correct or incorrect unless it is obvious.
- *Move rapidly* from concept to concept as soon as students have grasped the main idea.
- *Maintain momentum* by eliminating interruptions, asking many questions, and moving rapidly through the lesson.

After teaching the lesson, announce team assignments and have students move their desks together to make team tables. Tell students that they will be working in teams for several weeks and competing for recognition in a class newsletter.

Note: The first week of STAD is the hardest, but by the second week most students will settle into the pattern. Some students may complain about the teams to which they are assigned, but by the second week almost all such students find a way to get along with their teammates. *Do not* change team assignments after announcing them except under extreme circumstances, because it is students' realization that they will be in their team for several weeks that motivates them to work on getting along with their teammates instead of complaining about them. After five or six weeks of STAD, however, reassigning students to new teams may be helpful because this will give those who were on low-scoring teams a new chance, allow all students to work with other classmates, and keep the program fresh.

TEAM STUDY

Time: One to two class periods
Main Idea: **Students study worksheets in their teams to master the material.**
Materials Needed:
- Two *worksheets* for every *team*
- *Two answer sheets* for every *team*

During team study, the team members' tasks are to master the material presented in the lesson and to help their teammates master the material. Students have worksheets and answer sheets that they can use to practice the skill being taught and to assess themselves and their teammates. Each team receives only two copies of each worksheet and answer sheet in order to force teammates to work together, but if some students prefer to work alone or want their own copy, make additional copies available. During team study:

- Have teammates move their desks together or move to team tables.
- *Hand out* worksheets and answer sheets (two of each per team) with a minimum of fuss.

27

- Tell students *to work together in twos or threes.* If they are working problems (as in math), each student in a two- or threesome should work the problem and then check with his or her partner(s). If anyone misses a question, his or her teammates are responsible for explaining it. Students who are working on short-answer questions may quiz each other, with partners taking turns holding the answer sheet or attempting to answer the questions.
- Emphasize to students that they have not finished studying until they are *sure their teammates will make 100 percent* on the quiz.
- Make sure that students understand that the worksheets are for *studying,* not for filling out and handing in. For this reason it is important that students have the answer sheets to check themselves and their teammates as they study.
- Have students *explain* answers to each other instead of just checking each other against the answer sheet.
- When students have questions, have them *ask a teammate* before asking the teacher.
- While students are working in teams, *circulate among the class,* praising teams that are working well, sitting in with each team to hear how it is doing.

TEST

Time: One-half to one class period
Main Idea: **Students take individual quizzes.**
Materials Needed: One Quiz Sheet per student

- Distribute Quiz Sheets and give students adequate time to complete them. *Do not let students work together on the quiz;* at this point they must show what they have learned as individuals. Have students move their desks apart if possible.
- Either allow students to *exchange papers* with members of other teams, or *collect the quizzes* to score after class. Be sure to have the quizzes scored and team scores figured in time for the next class if at all possible.

TEAM RECOGNITION

Main Ideas: **Compute team scores based on team members' individual improvement scores and recognize high-scoring teams in a class newsletter or bulletin board.**

Figuring individual and team scores. As soon as possible after each quiz, figure individual improvement scores and team scores and write a class newsletter (or prepare a class bulletin board) to announce the team scores. If at all possible, announce the team scores in the first period after the quiz. This makes the connection between doing well and receiving recognition clear to students, which increases their motivation to do their best.

Improvement points. The points that students earn for their teams are the differences between their quiz scores and their base scores (as determined and entered on the Quiz Score Sheet while getting ready for STAD). Note that this system is based on 30-item quizzes, which are used in all the Johns Hopkins Team Learning materials. Teachers using their own quizzes, or dividing one of the Johns Hopkins quizzes into two or more shorter ones, must adjust scores to equal those of a 30-item quiz. For example, each item on a 10-item quiz is worth 3 points, each item on a 15-item quiz is worth 2 points, and each item on a 20-item quiz is worth $1^1/2$ points. Students can earn a maximum of 10 improvement points, and they receive the 10-point maximum for a perfect paper, regardless of their base score. The purpose of the maximum is to avoid putting an unfair ceiling on the possible scores of high-performing students. The minimum number of improvement points that students can earn is zero (even if their quiz scores are below their base). Thus, a column of the Quiz Score Sheet could be filled out as shown in Figure 4.

Figure 4: **Example of Base Scores and Improvement Points**

Quiz: Adding two digits without renaming

Student	Base Score	Quiz Score	Improvement Points
John	16	23	7
Mary	18	30	10
Tanya	23	30	10
Sam	16	27	10
Cheryl	17	17	0
Jose	21	23	2
Frank	18	17	0

Note that the improvement points are simply the difference between the quiz score and the base score, with a few exceptions. Mary and Sam would have earned more than 10 improvement points, but 10 is the maximum. Frank did not even make his base score, but he does not get negative improvement points—just zero. Figuring improvement points is not difficult, and with a little practice, it takes only a few minutes. The purpose of base scores and improvement points is to enable all students to bring maximum points to their teams, whatever their level of past performance. Students understand that it is fair that each one should be compared with his or her own level of past performance, as all students enter class with different levels of skills and experience on the subject.

Place the points you have calculated on each student's quiz: for example, Base Score = 18; Quiz Score = 23; Improvement Points = 5.

Team scores. To figure team scores, enter each student's improvement points on the appropriate Team Summary Sheet. For four-member teams, simply add the individual improvement points to find the team scores; for two-, three-, or five-member teams, however, use Appendix A (see chapter 4) to prorate the total team scores to be comparable with those of the four-member teams. For example, if a five-member team had a total score of 25, its transformed score would be 20. Consider only the transformed score in determining the team standing and computing the cumulative score. Figure 5 shows two STAD team score sheets. Note that in the four-member team (Fantastic Four), the scores were simply added to find the total team score; in the five-member team (Five Alive), the score was prorated using Appendix A.

Recognizing team accomplishments. Newsletters are the primary means for providing team recognition, but depending on the class, bulletin boards and other rewards are also useful and important.

Newsletters. As soon as possible after calculating each student's improvement points and figuring team scores, write a newsletter to recognize successful teams. These can be written on one ditto master and class copies run off. In the newsletter, emphasize team success as much as possible. For example, in mentioning students who received maximum scores (10 points), always mention their teams. It is important to help students value team success. The teacher's own enthusiasm about team scores will help. If students take more than one quiz in a week, combine the quiz results into a single weekly newsletter report. Figure 6 shows a sample STAD newsletter. Note that the score of the five-member Five Alive team is represented with the total score, a slash, and the transformed score.

Bulletin boards. Instead of or in addition to newsletters, bulletin boards may be used to recognize team success. Many teachers write the team names on strips of construction paper or poster board and display them in order of team standings on the last quiz. For example, one teacher put the team names on kites and arranged them so that the highest team was the highest kite; another put the team names on pictures of flowers and used the height of the flower to represent the team standing.

Other rewards. The amount and kind of reward teachers give for team success will help determine the success of STAD, but different classes need different amounts or kinds. In many schools, especially those that have many students with motivation problems, it may be crucial to give the winning teams something more than (or instead of) the newsletter. For the top three teams, it could be refreshments, free time during class to play quiet board games or read, ribbons or trophies, permission to line up first for recess or to go to the next class, or some other inexpensive reward of value to students. The rewards need not be large to be quite important in convincing students that the teacher really values team success, although teacher attitude toward cooperation and team success will be more important that any amount of team reward.

Returning the first set of quizzes. When students receive the first set of quizzes with base scores, quiz scores, and improvement points, they will need an explanation of the improvement point system:

- The main purpose of the improvement point system is to give everyone a minimum score to try to beat and to set that minimum score based on past performance so that all students will have an equal chance to be successful if they do their best academically.
- The second purpose of the improvement point system is to make students realize that the scores of everyone on their team are important, that all team members can earn maximum improvement points if they do their best.
- The improvement point system is fair because everyone is competing only with himself or herself—trying to improve individual performance—regardless of what the rest of the class docs.

Recomputing base scores after two quizzes. The initial assignment of base scores is just a beginning point. After the first two quizzes, it will be necessary to use Appendix B (see Chapter 4) to determine each student's new base score. To do this, add each student's two quiz scores, and find the total score in the left-hand column of the table. Then find the old base score at the top of the table. Follow the row across and the column down to the point where they intersect. This will be the student's new base score. For example, suppose a student had a base score of 18 and quiz scores of 23 and 28, making a total quiz score of 51. Looking at Appendix B, first find the number 51. Looking at Appendix B, first find the number 51 in the left-hand column of the table. Then find the old base score (18) along the top of the table. At the intersection of this row and column is the number 20, which is the student's new base score. If a student has missed a quiz, double the one quiz score that is available and then use the table in the same way. If the student has missed both quizzes, give the student the old base score again. If a student receives a zero for skipping class or for some disciplinary reason, be sure to count it as a missed quiz for the purpose of assigning base scores.

Students should know their own base scores but not those of other students. They should learn their base scores on a returned quiz or in some other private way.

Grading. Report card grades should be based on the students' actual quiz scores, not on improvement points or team scores. However, students' improvement points and/or team scores can be made a small part of their grades; or, if the school gives separate grades for effort, these scores can be used to determine the effort grades.

Figure 5: Examples of STAD Team Scores

TEAM SUMMARY SHEET

Team Name Fantastic Four

Team Members	1	2	3	4	5	6	7	8	9	10
Frank	8	10	8							
Otis	10	7	6							
Ursula	0	3	10							
Rebecca	7	10	10							
Total Team Score	25	30	34							
Transformed Team Score	—	—	—							
Team Standing This Week	2	1	2							
Cumulative Score	25	55	29							
Cumulative Standing	2	1	1							

TEAM SUMMARY SHEET

Team Name The Five Alive

Team Members	1	2	3	4	5	6	7	8	9	10
Carlos	10	5	10							
Irene	6	1	4							
Nancy	10	10	6							
Charles	4	5	10							
Oliver	0	4	7							
Total Team Score	30	25	37							
Transformed Team Score	24	20	30							
Team Standing This Week	5	7	5							
Cumulative Score	24	44	74							
Cumulative Standing	5	6	5							

Figure 6: **Sample STAD Newsletter**

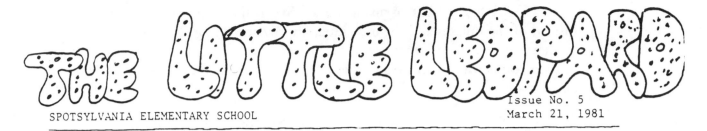

SPOTSYLVANIA ELEMENTARY SCHOOL

Issue No. 5
March 21, 1981

CALCULATORS OUTFIGURE CLASS!

The Calculators (Charlene, Alfredo, Laura, and Carl) calculated their way into first place this week, with big ten-point scores by Charlene, Alfredo, and Carl, and a near-perfect team score of 38! Their score jumped them from sixth to third in cumulative rank. Way to go Calcs! The Fantastic Four (Frank, Otis, Ursula, and Rebecca) also did a fantastic job, with Ursula and Rebecca turning in ten-pointers, but the Tigers (Cissy, Lindsay, Arthur, and Willy) clawed their way from last place last week to a tie with the red-hot Four, who were second the first week, and first last week. The Fantastic Four stayed in first place in cumulative rank. The Tigers were helped out by ten-point scores from Lindsay and Arthur. The Math Monsters (Gary, Helen, Octavia, Ulysses, and Luis) held on to fourth place this week, but due to their big first-place score in the first week they're still in second place in overall rank. Helen and Luis got ten points to help the M.M.'s. Just behind the Math Monsters were the Five Alive (Carlos, Irene, Nancy, Charles, and Oliver), with ten point scores by Carlos and Charles, and then in order the Little Professors, Fractions, and Brains. Susan turned in ten points for the L.P.'s as did Linda for the Brains.

- -

This Week's Rank	This Week's Score	Overall Score	Overall Rank
1st - Calculators	38	81	3
2nd - Fantastic Four ⎫ Tie	35	89	1
2nd - Tigers ⎭	35	73	6
4th - Math Monsters	40/32	85	2
5th - Five Alive	37/30	74	5
6th - Little Professors	26	70	8
7th - Fractions	23	78	4
8th - Brains	22	71	7

- -

TEN POINT SCORERS

Charlene	(Calculators)	Helen	(Math Monsters)
Alfredo	(Calculators)	Luis	(Math Monsters)
Carl	(Calculators)	Carlos	(Five Alive)
Ursula	(Fantastic Four)	Charles	(Five Alive)
Rebecca	(Fantastic Four)	Susan	(Little Professors)
Lindsay	(Tigers)	Linda	(Brains)
Arthur	(Tigers)		

TEAMS-GAMES-TOURNAMENT

TGT, like STAD, is made up of five major components. However, instead of the quizzes and the individual improvement score system, TGT uses academic games and tournaments, in which students compete as representatives of their teams with members of other teams who are like them in past academic performance.

1. **Class presentations.** The teacher initially introduces the material in a class presentation. In most cases, this is a lecture/discussion, but it can include an audiovisual presentation. Class presentations in Teams-Games-Tournament differ from usual teaching only in that they must clearly focus on the TGT unit. Thus students realize that they must pay careful attention during the presentation because doing so will help them do well on the quizzes, and their quiz scores determine their team scores.

2. **Teams.** Teams are composed of four or five students who represent a cross-section of the class in academic performance, sex, and race or ethnicity. The major function of the team is to prepare its members to do well on the quizzes. After the teacher presents the material, the team meets to study worksheets or other material. The worksheets may be obtained from the Johns Hopkins Team Learning Project (see the preface for the address), or they may be teacher-made materials (see Chapter 4, Appendix C). Most often, the study takes the form of students quizzing one another to be sure that they understand the content, or of students working problems together and correcting any misconceptions that may have caused teammates to make mistakes.

   The team is the most important feature of TGT. At every point, the emphases are on the members doing their best for the team and on the team doing its best for the members. The team provides important peer support for academic performance; it also provides the mutual concern and respect that are important for producing such outcomes as improved intergroup relations, self-esteem, and acceptance of mainstreamed students.

3. **Games.** The games are composed of simple, course-content-relevant questions that students must answer, and they are designed to test the knowledge students gain from class presentations and team practice. Games are played at tables of three students, each of whom represents a different team. Most games are simply numbered questions on a ditto sheet. A student picks a number card and attempts to answer the question corresponding to the number. A challenge rule permits players to challenge each other's answers.

4. **Tournament.** The tournament is the structure in which the

games take place. It is usually held at the end of the week, after the teacher has made a class presentation and the teams have had time to practice with the worksheets. For the first tournament, the teacher assigns students to tournament tables: the top three students in past performance to Table 1, the next three to Table 2, and so on. This equal competition, like the individual improvement score system in STAD, makes it possible for students of all levels of past performance to contribute maximally to their team scores if they do their best. Figure 7 illustrates the relationship between heterogeneous teams and homogeneous tournament tables. After the first week, however, students change tables depending on their own performance in the most recent tournament. The winner at each table is "bumped up" to the next higher table (e.g., from Table 6 to Table 5), the second scorer stays at the same table, and the low scorer is "bumped down." In this way, if students have been misassigned at first, they will eventually be moved up or down until they reach their true level of performance.

Figure 7: **Assignment to Tournament Tables (TGT)**

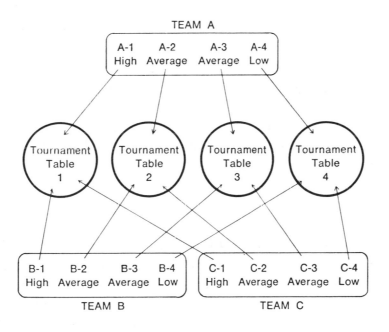

5. **Team recognition.** A newsletter is the primary means of rewarding teams and individual students for their performance. Each week the teacher prepares a newsletter to announce team scores. The newsletter also recognizes individuals showing the greatest improvement or completing perfect papers, and reports

cumulative team standings. In addition to or instead of the newsletter, many teachers use bulletin boards, special privileges, small prizes, or other rewards to emphasize the idea that doing well as a team is important.

Teachers may wish to use TGT for part of their instruction, and other methods for other parts. For example, a science teacher might use TGT three days a week to teach basic science concepts but then use related laboratory exercises on the other two days. TGT can also be used in combination with STAD, either by alternating quizzes one week and tournaments the next, or by having a quiz on the day after each tournament and counting both the quiz score and the tournament score toward the team score. This procedure gives the teacher a better idea of student progress than the tournament alone.

Getting Ready for Teams-Games-Tournament

Prepare Materials

TGT (like STAD) can be used either with curriculum materials specifically designed for Student Team Learning and distributed by the Johns Hopkins Team Learning Project (see the preface for the address) or with teacher-made materials (see Chapter 4, Appendix C for instructions). Currently, Johns Hopkins materials are available in grade two through eight mathematics; high school consumer mathematics, algebra I, and geometry; elementary and junior high school language arts; elementary and secondary school nutrition; and junior high school life science, physical science, and U.S. history.

For each unit, which should take from three to five days of instruction, a worksheet, a worksheet answer sheet, a game, and a game answer sheet are needed. Also needed is one set of cards numbered from 1 to 30 for every three students in the largest class.

Assign Students to Teams

A Teams-Games-Tournament team consists of four or five students who represent a cross-section of the class in terms of sex, race or ethnicity, and past performance. Thus, in a class that is one-half male, one-half female, three-quarters white, and one-quarter minority, a four-person team should include two boys and two girls, of which three are white and one is minority. The team should also include one high performer, one low performer, and two average performers. Of course, "high" and "low" are relative terms, relating to high and low for the class rather than to high or low compared to national norms.

It is the teacher who should assign students to teams, taking into account student likes, dislikes, and "deadly combinations" as well as criteria for a representative class cross-section. The following steps should be used:

Step 1: **Copy Team Summary and Game Score Sheets from Appendix E (in Chapter 4).** Before assigning students to teams, make one copy of a Team Summary Sheet for every four students in the class and one copy of a Game Score Sheet for every team for every three weeks that TGT will be used.

Step 2: **Rank students.** On a sheet of paper, rank students in the class from highest to lowest in terms of past performance. Use whatever information is available: test scores, grades, teacher judgment. If exact ranking is difficult, do the best you can.

Step 3: **Decide on the number of teams.** Each team should have four members if possible. Divide the number of students in the class by four. If the division is even, the quotient will be the number of teams to have. For example, a class of 32 students will have eight four-member teams. If the division is uneven, the remainder will be one, two, or three, so that there may be one, two, or three teams composed of five members. For example, a class of 30 students will have seven teams—five with four members and two with five members.

Step 4: **Assign students to teams.** First, balance the teams according to *performance:* Each team should be composed of students whose performance levels range from low to average to high; and the average performance level of all teams in the class should be approximately equal. Thus students with different performance levels will be able to tutor each other; and no single team will have an advantage in terms of academic performance.

Use the list of students ranked by performance made in Step 2 and assign team letters to each student. For example, in an eight-team class, use the eight letters A through H, as in Figure 3, starting at the top with the letter A. After using the last team letter, continue lettering but in the opposite order. In Figure 3, the students ranked eighth, ninth, twenty-sixth, and twenty-seventh comprise the H team; the students ranked first, sixteenth, nineteenth, and thirty-fourth go on the A team. Note that the students ranked seventeenth and eighteenth are not yet assigned. They will be assigned to teams as fifth members.

Now check the teams for sex and race or ethnicity balance. For example, when one-fourth of a class is Black, approximately one student on each team should be Black; and when a class has more than two major ethnic groups, their proportions should be reflected in team membership. If teams balanced by performance are not balanced by race or ethnicity and sex—and they rarely are on the first try—trade students of the same approximate performance level among teams and place fifth members as available and needed until there is a balance.

Step 5: **Fill in the names of the students on Team Summary Sheets,** leaving the team name blank, after assigning all students to teams. If there are six or more teams, divide them into two leagues. (Many teachers name the two leagues—e.g., American and National.)

Assign Students to Initial Tournament Tables

Make a copy of the Tournament Table Assignment Sheet from Appendix E (see Chapter 4). On it, list students from top to bottom in past performance in the same ranking used to form teams. Count the number of students in the class. If the number is divisible by three, all tournament tables will have three members; assign the first three students on the list to Table 1, the next three to Table 2, and so on. If the division has a remainder, one or two of the top tournament tables will have four members. For example, a class of 29 students will have nine tournament tables, two of which will have four members (29 divided by 3 = 9 r 2). The first four students on the ranked list will be assigned to Table 1, the next four to Table 2, and three to other tables.

Activities

As shown in Figure 1, Teams-Games-Tournament consists of regular cycles of instructional activities: teach, team study, tournament, and team recognition.

TEACH

Time: One to two class periods
Main Idea: **Present the lesson.**
Materials Needed: Lesson plan

Each lesson in TGT begins with a class presentation. A filmstrip or movie or other technique can be used to introduce the lesson, but most teachers simply give a lecture/discussion. In the lesson, stress the following (adapted from Good and Grouws 1979):

- *Briefly review* any prerequisite skills or information.
- Stick close to the *objectives* that you will test.
- Focus on *meaning*, not memorization.
- Actively *demonstrate* concepts or skills, using visual aids and many examples.
- Frequently *assess* student comprehension by asking many questions.
- Have all students *work problems* or *prepare* answers to your questions.
- Call on students *at random* so that they will never know who is going to have to answer a question. This makes all students prepare themselves to answer. *Do not* just call on students who raise their hands.
- *Do not give long class assignments* at this point. For example, have students work one or two problems or prepare one or two answers and then give them feedback.

- Always *explain* why an answer is correct or incorrect unless it is obvious.
- *Move rapidly* from concept to concept as soon as students have grasped the main idea.
- *Maintain momentum* by eliminating interruptions, asking many questions, and moving rapidly through the lesson.

After teaching the lesson, announce team assignments and have students move their desks together to make team tables. Tell students that they will be working in teams for several weeks and competing in academic games to add points to their team scores, and that the highest-scoring teams will receive recognition in a class newsletter.

Note: The first week of TGT is the hardest, but by the second week most students will settle into the pattern. Some students may complain about the teams to which they are assigned, but by the second week almost all such students find a way to get along with their teammates. *Do not* change team assignments after announcing them except under extreme circumstances because it is students' realization that they will be in their team for several weeks that motivates them to work on getting along with their teammates instead of complaining about them.

After five or six weeks of TGT, however, assign students to new teams.

TEAM STUDY

Time: One to two class periods
Main Idea: **Students study worksheets in their teams to master the material.**
Materials Needed:
- Two *worksheets* for every *team*
- Two *answer sheets* for every *team*

During team study, the team members' tasks are to master the material presented in the lesson and to help their teammates master the material. Students have worksheets and answer sheets that they can use to practice the skill being taught and to assess themselves and their teammates. Each team receives only two copies of each worksheet and answer sheet in order to force teammates to work together, but if some students prefer to work alone or want their own copy, make additional copies available. During team study:

- Have teammates move their desks together or move to team tables.
- *Hand out* worksheets and answer sheets (two of each per team) with a minimum of fuss.
- Tell students *to work together in twos or threes.* If they are working problems (as in math), each student in a two- or threesome should work the problem and then check with his or her partner(s). If anyone misses a question, his or her teammates are responsible for explaining

it. Students who are working on short-answer questions may quiz each other, with partners taking turns holding the answer sheet or attempting to answer the questions.

- Emphasize to students that they have not finished studying until they are *sure their teammates will make 100 percent* on the quiz.
- Make sure that students understand that the worksheets are for *studying*, not for filling out and handing in. For this reason it is important that students have the answer sheets to check themselves and their teammates as they study.
- Have students *explain* answers to each other instead of just checking each other against the answer sheet.
- When students have questions, have them *ask a teammate* before asking the teacher.
- While students are working in teams, *circulate among the class,* praising teams that are working well, sitting in with each team to hear how it is doing.

TOURNAMENT

Time: One class period

Main Idea: **Students play academic games in three-member, ability-homogeneous tournament tables.**

Materials Needed:

- Tournament Table Assignment Sheet, with tournament table assignments filled in
- One copy of a Game Sheet and a Game Answers Sheet (same as the quiz sheet and quiz answers for STAD) for each tournament table
- One Game Score Sheet (copy from Appendix E, Chapter 4) for each tournament table
- One deck of number cards for each tournament table.

At the beginning of the tournament period, announce students' tournament table assignments and have them move desks together or go to tables serving as tournament tables. Have selected students help distribute one Game Sheet, one Game Answers Sheet, and one Game Score Sheet to each table. Then begin the game. Figure 8 describes the game rules and procedures.

To start the game, the students draw cards to determine the first reader—the student drawing the highest number. Play proceeds in a clockwise direction from the first reader.

When the game begins, the reader shuffles the cards and picks the top one. He or she then reads aloud the question corresponding to the number on the card, including the possible answers if the question is multiple choice. For example, a student who picks card number 21 answers question number 21. A reader who is not sure of the answer is allowed to guess without penalty. If the

40

Reader

1. Picks a numbered card and finds the corresponding question on the game sheet.
2. Reads the question out loud.
3. Tries to answer.

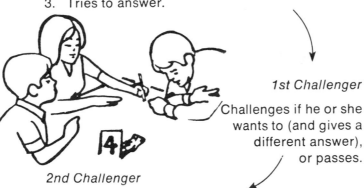

1st Challenger

Challenges if he or she wants to (and gives a different answer), or passes.

2nd Challenger

Challenges if 1st challenger passes, if he or she wants to. When all have challenged or passed, 2nd challenger checks the answer sheet. Whoever was *right* keeps the card. If the *reader* was wrong, there is no penalty, but if either challenger was wrong, he or she must put a previously won card, if any, back in the deck.

content of the game involves math problems, all students (not just the reader) should work the problems so that they will be ready to challenge. After the reader gives an answer, the student to his left (first challenger) has the option of challenging and giving a different answer. If her or she passes, or if the second challenger has an answer different from that of the first two, the second challenger may challenge. Challengers have to be careful, however, because they lose a card (if they have one) if they are wrong. When everyone has answered, challenged, or passed, the second challenger checks the answer sheet and reads the right answer aloud. The player who gave the right answer keeps the card. If either challenger gave a wrong answer, he or she must return a previously won card (if any) to the deck. If no one gave a right answer, the card returns to the deck.

For the next round, everything moves one position to the left: the first challenger becomes the reader, the second challenger becomes the first challenger, and the reader becomes the second challenger. Play continues until the period ends or the deck is exhausted. When the game is over, players record the number of cards they won on the Game Score Sheet in the column marked Game 1. If there is time, students reshuffle the deck and play a second game until the end of the period, recording the number of cards won in the column marked Game 2 on the score sheet, as shown in Figure 9.

Figure 9: Sample Game Score Sheet (TGT)

TABLE # ___	GAME SCORE SHEET (TGT)				ROUND # ___	
Player	Team	Game 1	Game 2	Game 3	Day's Total	Tournament Points
ERIC	GIANTS	5	7		12	2
LISA A.	GENIUSES	14	10		24	6
DARRYL	B. BOMBS	11	12		23	4

Figure 10: Calculating Tournament Points (TGT)

FOR A FOUR-PLAYER GAME

Player	No Ties	Tie For Top	Tie For Middle	Tie For Low	3-Way Tie For Top	3-Way Tie For Low	4-Way Tie	Tie For Low and High
Top Scorer	6 points	5	6	6	5	6	4	5
High Middle Scorer	4 points	5	4	4	5	3	4	5
Low Middle Scorer	3 points	3	4	3	5	3	4	3
Low Scorer	2 points	2	2	3	2	3	4	3

FOR A THREE-PLAYER GAME

Player	No Ties	Tie For Top Score	Tie For Low Score	3-Way Tie
Top Scorer	6 points	5	6	4
Middle Scorer	4 points	5	3	4
Low Scorer	2 points	2	3	4

FOR A TWO-PLAYER GAME

Player	No Ties	Tied
Top Scorer	6 points	4
Low Scorer	2 points	4

Figure 11: **Bumping in TGT**

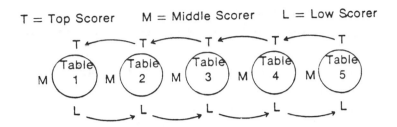

All students should play the game at the same time. While they are playing, the teacher should move from group to group to answer questions and be sure that everyone understands the game procedures. Ten minutes before the end of the period, time should be called. Students should stop, count their cards, and then fill in their names, teams and scores on the Game Score Sheet, as shown in Figure 9.

Have students add up the scores they earned in each game (if they played more than one) and fill in their day's total. For younger children (fourth grade or below), simply collect the score sheets. If students are older, have them calculate their tournament points. Figure 10 summarizes tournament points for all possible outcomes. In general, have students give the top scorer 6 points, the second scorer 4 points, and the third scorer 2 points at a three-person table with no ties. If there are more or less than three players or if there are any ties, use Figure 10 to tell students what to do. When everyone has calculated his or her tournament points, have a student collect the Game Score Sheets.

Bumping: Reassigning students to tournament tables. Bumping, or reassigning students to new tournament tables, must be done after each tournament to prepare for the next tournament. It is easiest to do the bumping when figuring team scores and writing the newsletter.

To "bump" students, use the steps that follow. Figure 11 shows a diagram of the bumping procedures, and Figure 12 gives an example of a completed Tournament Table Assignment Sheet, showing how the bumping procedure works for a hypothetical class after two tournaments (one tournament per week).

Step 1: **Use the Game Score Sheets to identify the high and low scorers at each tournament table.** On the Tournament Table Assignment Sheet, circle the table assignments of all students who were high scorers at their tables. If there was a tie for high score at any table, flip a coin to decide which number to circle; do not circle more than one number per table. In Figure 12, Tyrone, Maria, Tom, Carla, and Ralph were table winners in the first tournament, so their table

43

numbers are circled in the first column; Tyrone, Liz, John T., Tanya, and Ruth were winners in the second tournament, so their numbers are circled in the second column.

Step 2: **Underline the table numbers of students who were low scorers.** Again, if there was a tie for low score at any table, flip a coin to decide which to underline; do not underline more than one number per table. In Figure 12, Sarah, John T., John F., Kim, and Shirley were low scorers at their respective tables in the first tournament; Sam, Sylvia, Tom, John F., and Kim were low scorers in the second tournament.

Step 3: **Leave all other table assignments as they were,** including numbers for absent students

Step 4: **In the column for the next tournament, transfer the numbers** as follows:

If the number is *circled,* reduce it by one (④ becomes 3). This means that the winner at Table 4 will compete at Table 3 the next week, a table where the competition will be more difficult. The only exception is that ① remains 1, because Table 1 is the highest table. If the number is *underlined,* increase it by one (4 becomes 5), except at the lowest table, where the low scorer stays at the same table (e.g., 10 remains 10). This means that the low scorer at each table will compete the next week at a table where the competition will be less difficult. If the number is neither underlined nor circled, do not change it for the next tournament—transfer the same number.

In Figure 12, note that Tom won at Table 3 in the first tournament and was bumped up to Table 2. At Table 2 he was the low scorer, so for the third week's tournament he will compete at Table 3 again. Sylvia was the middle scorer at Table 3 in the first tournament, so she stayed at Table 3; then she lost in the second tournament and was moved to Table 4.

Step 5: **Count the number of students assigned to each table for the next week's tournament.** Most tables should have three students; as many as two may have four. If table assignments do not work out this way, make some changes so that they do.

Note that in Figure 12, Tyrone won twice at Table 1 but did not change tables because there was no higher place to go than Table 1. Shirley and Kim lost at Table 5 but were not "bumped down" because Table 5 was the lowest table.

TEAM RECOGNITION

Main Ideas: **Compute team scores based on team members' tournament scores, and prepare a class newsletter or bulletin board recognizing high-scoring teams.**

Figure 12: Sample Tournament Table Assignment Sheet with Bumping (TGT)

TOURNAMENT TABLE ASSIGNMENT SHEET (TGT) (Five Tournament Tables)

Tournament Number:

Student	Team	1	2	3	4	5	6	7	8	9	10	11	12	13
SAM	Orioles	1	_1_	2										
SARAH	Cougars	_1_	2	2										
TYRONE	Whiz Kids	①	①	1										
MARIA	Geniuses	②	1	1										
LIZ	Orioles	2	②	1										
JOHN T.	Cougars	2	③	2										
SYLVIA	Whiz Kids	3	_3_	4										
TOM	Geniuses	③	2	3										
JOHN F.	Orioles	_3_	4	5										
TANYA	Whiz Kids	4	④	3										
CARLA	Orioles	④	3	3										
KIM	Cougars	4	5	5										
CARLOS	Geniuses	4	4	4										
SHIRLEY	Whiz Kids	_5_	5	5										
RALPH	Cougars	⑤	4	4										
RUTH	Geniuses	5	⑤	4										

Note:
③ indicates *high* scorer at Table 3
3 indicates *middle* scorer at Table 3
<u>3</u> indicates *low* scorer at Table 3

Results of Most Recent Tournament ↑   ↑ Tournament Table Assignment for Next Tournament

45

Figuring team scores. As soon as possible after the tournament, figure team scores and write the class newsletter to announce the standings. To do this, first check the tournament points on the Game Score Sheets. Then simply transfer each student's tournament points to the Team Summary Sheet for his or her team, and add all the team members' scores. If the team has four members, the scoring is finished. However, if the team has more or fewer members than four, it will be necessary to transform the scores in order to compare team scores fairly. Appendix A (see Chapter 4) gives transformed scores for all possible team sizes and number of points. For example, a five-member team with a total of 22 will receive a transformed score of 18. Consider only the transformed scores for three- or five-member teams in determining the team rank. Also record the cumulative team score to date on the Team Summary Sheet. Use the transformed score, of course, to figure the cumulative score.

Figure 13 shows the recording and totaling of scores for one team. Note that because this team has five members, the total team scores have been transformed to be comparable with those of four-member teams.

Figure 13: **Sample Team Summary Sheet (TGT)**

Team Name GENIUSES

Team Members	1	2	3	4	5	6	7	8	9	10
MARK	6	2	2	4						
KEVIN	4	4	2	6						
LISA A.	5	2	4	6						
JOHN F.	6	6	2	4						
DEWANDA	4	4	6	2						
Total Team Score	25	18	16	22						
Transformed Team Score	20	14	13	18						
Team Standing This Week	1	3	5	3						
Cumulative Score	20	34	47	65						
Cumulative Standing	1	1	2	2						

Recognizing team accomplishments. The motivational force that TGT generates is greatly enhanced by the use of public announcements, bulletin board displays, and newsletters to publicize the tournament results and indicate their importance. Of the three, the newsletter is perhaps the most effective method of creating a sense of excitement about the tournament and the students' performance.

The newsletter is also easy to produce. It can be written or typed on a ditto master and then run off and distributed to each student. It is important to distribute the newsletter as soon as possible after each tournament.

Once the Team Summary Sheets are completed (see Figure 13), it is easy to transfer the information for the last recorded tournament into a newsletter format. The Team Summary Sheets contain columns for several tournaments. After the sheets are completed, it is simply a matter of sorting them, once to rank the team scores for the latest tournament from highest to lowest, and once to rank the cumulative team scores. Transfer the information to the newsletter.

Figure 14 depicts a sample TGT newsletter. Note that although this newsletter emphasizes team success, it also recognizes table winners, along with their teams. Rewards for winning teams such as refreshments, free time, or special privileges may be added to the newsletter recognition to make team success more important to students. (See the discussion of such additional rewards in the section on STAD.

Grading. TGT does not automatically produce scores that can be used to compute individual grades. If this is a serious problem, consider using STAD instead of TGT. To determine individual grades, many teachers using TGT give a midterm and a final test each semester; some give a quiz after each tournament. Students' grades should be based on quiz scores or other individual assessments, not on tournament points or team scores. However, students' tournament points and/or team scores can be made a small part of their grades; or if the school gives separate grades for effort, these scores can be used to determine the effort grades.

JIGSAW II

Jigsaw II can be used whenever the material to be studied is in written narrative form. It is most appropriate in such subjects as social studies, literature, some parts of science, and related areas in which concepts rather than skills are the learning goals. The instructional raw material for Jigsaw II should usually be a chapter, a story, a biography, or similar narrative or descriptive material.

In Jigsaw II, students work in heterogeneous teams as in STAD and TGT. Students are assigned chapters or other units to read and are given an Expert Sheet that contains different topics for each team member to focus on when reading. When everyone has finished reading, students from different teams with the same topic meet in an expert group to discuss their topic for about 30 minutes. The experts then return to their teams and take turns teaching their teammates about their topics. Finally, students take quizzes that cover all the topics, and the quiz scores become team scores as in STAD. Also as in STAD, the scores that students contribute to their teams are based on the individual improvement score system, and high-scoring teams and individuals are recognized in a newsletter or bulletin board. Thus, students are motivated to study the material well and to work hard in their expert groups so that they can help their team do well. The key to Jigsaw is interdependence: every student

Figure 14: **Sample TGT Newsletter**

The Weekly Planet

4th Week March 28

FLASH! Fantastic Four Sweeps Language Arts Tournament!

The Fantastic Four was the winning team this week with a total of 22 points. John T., Kris, and Alvin put in outstanding performances for the Four, each contributing six points to their team. Their victory brings the Four to second place in the National League standings, only six points behind the leading Giants!

Hot on the heels of the Fantastic Four were the Brain Busters with 21 points. Anita and Tanya helped the team out with victories at their tables, while Peter tied for first at his. The Brain Busters are still in third place in National League competition, but are moving up fast!

Third this week were the American League Geniuses with 18 points. They were helped out by Kevin and Lisa A., both table winners. Other table winners were Lisa P. of the Daredevils and Mike of the Grammar Haters.

THIS WEEK'S SCORES

1ST--Fantastic Four		2ND--Brain Busters		3RD--Geniuses	
John T.	6	Anita	6	Mark	4
Mary	4	Peter	5	Kevin	6
Kris	6	Darryl	4	Lisa A.	6
Alvin	6	Tanya	6	John F.	4
	22		21	Dewanda	2
					22/18

Daredevils		Giants		Chipmunks		Grammar Haters	
Lisa P.	6	Robert	4	Caroline	5	Sarah	2
Henry	2	Eric	2	Jerry	2	Willy	2
Cindi	4	Sharon	2	Charlene	3	Mike	6
Fred	4	Sylvia	4	James	2	Theresa	3
						John H.	2
	16		12		12		15/12

SEASON'S STANDING FOURTH WEEK

National League		American League	
TEAM	SEASON SCORE	TEAM	SEASON SCORE
Giants	78	Grammar Haters	74
Fantastic Four	72	Geniuses	65
Brain Busters	66	Daredevils	57
Chipmunks	59		

depends on teammates to provide the information he or she needs to do well on the quizzes.

Getting Ready to Use Jigsaw II

Prepare Materials

Before beginning, make an Expert Sheet and a quiz for each unit of material. At present, Johns Hopkins Team Learning Project materials are available for Jigsaw only in junior high school U.S. History, but preparing these materials is not difficult. Appendix D (see Chapter 4) presents an example of a complete Jigsaw II unit.

To make materials for Jigsaw II follow these steps:

Step 1: **Select several chapters, stories, or other units, each covering material for a two- to three-day unit.** If students are to read in class, the selections should not require more than a half hour to complete; if the reading is to be assigned for homework, the selections can be longer.

Step 2: **Make an Expert Sheet for each unit.** This tells students what to concentrate on while they read and which expert group they will work with. It identifies four topics that are central to the unit. For example, an Expert Sheet for a level four social studies book might refer to a section on the Blackfoot Indian tribes that is used to illustrate a number of concepts about groups, group norms, and leadership. The Expert Sheet for that section might be as follows:

Read: Pages 3-9 and 11-12
Topics:
1. How were Blackfoot men expected to act?
2. What is a group and what does it do?
   What are the most important groups for the Blackfoot?
3. What did Blackfoot bands and clubs do?
4. What were the Blackfoot customs and traditions?

As much as possible, the topics should cover themes that appear throughout the chapter instead of issues that appear only once. For example, if the class is reading *Tom Sawyer,* a good topic might be "How did Tom feel about his community?" (which appears throughout the book) as opposed to "What happened to Tom and Huck Finn when they ran away?" (which a student could learn by reading only a section of the book). For an example of topics based on Chapters 1 and 2 in this publication, see Appendix D (in Chapter 4). The expert topics may be put on ditto masters and one copy run off for each student, or they may be put on the chalkboard or poster paper.

Step 3: **Make a quiz for each unit.** The quiz should consist of at least eight questions (two for each topic) or some multiple of four (e.g., twelve,

49

sixteen, or twenty) so that there are an equal number of questions for each topic. Teachers may wish to add two or more general questions to give the quiz an even number of items. The questions should require considerable understanding because students will have had ample time to discuss their topics in depth, and easy questions would fail to challenge those who have done a good job in preparation. However, the questions should not be obscure. In the Blackfoot example, the first two questions might be as follows:

1A: Which of the following was *not* an expected way of behaving for a Blackfoot man?
   a. He was expected to be brave.
   b. He was expected to brag about how many of the enemy tribe he had touched.
   c. He was expected to clean buffalo meat.
   d. He was expected to share buffalo meat.

1B: What are norms of behavior?
   a. All the ways of acting that people in a group have
   b. The ways people in a group expect themselves and other members of the group to act
   c. Records of great deeds
   d. Sharing food with the very old

All students must answer all questions. The quiz should take no more than 10 minutes. Teachers may wish to use an activity other than a quiz or in addition to a quiz as an opportunity for team members to show their learning—for example, an oral report, a written report, a crafts project. A sample Jigsaw II quiz is included in Appendix D (see Chapter 4).

Step 4: **Use discussion outlines (optional).** A discussion outline for each topic can help guide the discussions in the expert groups. It should list the points that students need to consider in discussing their topics. For example, a discussion outline for a topic relating to the settlement of the English colonies in America is as follows:

Topic: What role did religious ideals play in the establishment of settlement in America?

Discussion outline:

—Puritan beliefs and religious practices
—Puritan treatment of disorders
—Founding of Connecticut and Rhode Island
—Quakers and the establishment of Pennsylvania
—Catholics and religious toleration in Maryland

Assign Students to Teams

A Jigsaw II team consists of four or five students who represent a cross-section of the class in terms of sex, race or ethnicity, and past performance.

Thus, in a class that is one-half male, one-half female, three-quarters white, and one-quarter minority, a four-person team should include two boys and two girls, of which three are white and one is minority. The team should also include one high performer, one low performer, and two average performers. Of course, "high" and "low" are relative terms, relating to high and low for the class rather than to high or low compared to national norms.

It is the teacher who should assign students to teams, taking into account student likes, dislikes, and "deadly combinations" as well as criteria for a representative class cross-section. The following steps should be used:

Step 1: **Copy Team Summary and Game Score Sheets from Appendix E (see Chapter 4).** Before assigning students to teams, make one copy of a Team Summary Sheet for every four students in the class and one copy of a Game Score Sheet for every team for every three weeks that Jigsaw II will be used.

Step 2: **Rank students.** On a sheet of paper, rank students in the class from highest to lowest in terms of past performance. Use whatever information is available: test scores, grades, teacher judgment. If exact ranking is difficult, do the best you can.

Step 3: **Decide on the number of teams.** Each team should have four members if possible. Divide the number of students in the class by four. If the division is even, the quotient will be the number of teams to have. For example, a class of 32 students will have eight four-member teams. If the division is uneven, the remainder will be one, two, or three, so that there may be one, two, or three teams composed of five members. For example, a class of 30 students will have seven teams—five with four members and two with five members.

Step 4: **Assign students to teams.** First, balance the teams according to *performance:* Each team should be composed of students whose performance levels range from low to average to high; and the average performance level of all teams in the class should be approximately equal. Thus students with different performance levels will be able to tutor each other; and no single team will have an advantage in terms of academic performance.

Use the list of students ranked by performance made in Step 2 and assign team letters to each student. For example, in an eight-team class, use the eight letters A through H, as in Figure 3, starting at the top with the letter A. After using the last team letter, continue lettering but in the opposite order. In Figure 3, the students ranked eighth, ninth, twenty-sixth, and twenty-seventh comprise the H team; the students ranked first, sixteenth, nineteenth, and thirty-fourth go on the A team. Note that the students ranked seventeenth and eighteenth are not yet assigned. They will be assigned to teams as fifth members. Now check the teams for sex and race or ethnicity balance. For

51

example, when one-fourth of a class is Black, approximately one student on each team should be Black; and when a class has more than two major ethnic groups, their proportions should be reflected in team membership. If teams balanced by performance are not balanced by race or ethnicity and sex—and they rarely are on the first try—trade students of the same approximate performance level among teams and place fifth members as available and needed until there is a balance.

Step 5: **Fill in the names of the students on Team Summary Sheets,** leaving the team name blank, after assigning all students to teams. If there are six or more teams, divide them into two leagues. (Many teachers name the two leagues—e.g., American and National.)

Determine Initial Base Scores

In addition to assigning students to teams, it is necessary to rank students on past performance and determine the initial base score for each student. A base score is the minimum the teacher expects the student to make, for example, on a 16-item quiz. Refer to the ranked list of students made in Step 2 of assigning students to teams: If the class has 25 or more students, give the first three students an initial base score of 20; the next three, 19; the next three, 18; and so on until you have assigned each student an initial base score. Put the base scores on a Quiz Score Sheet (see Appendix E in Chapter 4). If the class has 24 or fewer students, give the first two students an initial base score of 20; the next two, 19; and so on. Note that these base scores are just a start; they will be modified to reflect students' actual scores after every two quizzes. When these adjustments are made, the base score will eventually be set approximately 5 points below the student's average past quiz scores. If there are students at the very bottom of the list that the teacher feels have little chance of making even their base scores, their base scores should be set a little lower according to teacher judgment. Don't worry about setting base scores exactly; they will adjust themselves over time.

Activities

Jigsaw II consists of regular cycles of instructional activities: text, talk, team report, test, and team recognition.

TEXT

Time: One-half to one class period (or assign for homework)
Main Idea: **Students receive expert topics and read assigned material to locate information on their topics.**
Materials Needed:
- An Expert Sheet for each student, consisting of four expert topics
- A text or other reading assignment on which the expert topics for each student are based

Tell students that they will be working in teams for several weeks. Tell them that they will study different topics and teach their teams what they have learned, that the teams will be quizzed on all topics and the highest-scoring teams will be recognized in a class newsletter. Remember that the first week of Jigsaw II will be the hardest, but by the second week most students will settle into the pattern.

Distribute or assign a text or other reading. Pass out an Expert Sheet to each student. Announce team assignments. Randomly assign students on each team to take one of the four topics. If any team has five members, have two students take Expert Topic 1 together.

After the students have their team assignments and topics, let them read the materials. Or the reading may be assigned as homework. Students who finish reading before others can go back and make notes.

TALK

Time: One-half class period

Main Idea: **Students with the same expert topics discuss them in expert groups.**

Materials Needed:
- Expert Sheet and texts for each student
- (Optional) Discussion outlines for each topic; one for each student with that topic

Have all students with Expert Topic 1 get together at one table, all students with Expert Topic 2 at another, and so on. If any expert group has more than seven students (that is, if the class has more than 28 students), split the expert group into two smaller groups.

If students are to use a discussion outline, distribute it to each expert group.

Appoint a *discussion leader* for each group. The discussion leader need not be a particularly able student, and all students should have an opportunity to play that role at some time. The leader's job is to moderate the discussion, calling on group members who raise their hands and trying to see that everyone participates.

Give the expert groups about 20 minutes to discuss their topics. Students should try to locate information on their topics in their texts and share the information with the group. Group members should take notes on all points discussed.

While the expert groups are working, the teacher should circulate through the class, spending time with each group in turn. Teachers may wish to answer questions and resolve misunderstandings, but they should not try to take over leadership of the groups: that is the discussion leaders' responsibility. They may need to remind discussion leaders that part of their job is to see that everyone participates.

53

TEAM REPORT

Time: One-half class period

Main Idea: **Experts return to their teams to teach their topics to their teammates.**

Experts should return to their teams to teach their topics to their teammates. They should take about five minutes to review everything they have learned about their topics from their reading and their discussions in the expert groups.

If two students on any team shared Expert Topic 1, they should make a joint presentation.

Emphasize that students have a responsibility to their teammates to be good teachers as well as good listeners.

Teachers may hold a brief whole-class discussion after team reports are completed.

TEST

Time: One-half class period

Main Idea: **Students take individual quizzes covering all topics.**

Materials Needed: One copy of the quiz for each student

Distribute the quizzes and give students adequate time for almost everyone to finish. Have students exchange quizzes with members of other teams for scoring, or collect the quizzes for teacher scoring. If students do the scoring, have the checkers put their names at the bottom of the quizzes they checked. After class, spot check several quizzes to be sure that students did a good job of checking.

TEAM RECOGNITION

Main Ideas: **Compute team scores based on team members' individual improvement scores and recognize high-scoring teams in a class newsletter or bulletin board.**

Scoring for Jigsaw II is the same as that for STAD, including base scores, improvement points, and team scoring procedures. See the Team Recognition section of STAD for complete details. As in both STAD and TGT, newsletters, bulletin boards, and/or other rewards recognize high-scoring teams. Since Jigsaw units rarely have 30 items, it is necessary to give more than one point per item to stay close to 30 points for the quiz. (Approximately 30 points are needed to figure improvement scores.) Give the following number of points per item to make Jigsaw II quizzes approach 30 points:

Number of Quiz Items	Points per Item
8	4
12	$2^1/_2$
16	2
20	$1^1/_2$

Original Jigsaw

Aronson's original Jigsaw resembles Jigsaw II in most respects, but it also has some important differences. In the original Jigsaw, students read individual sections entirely different from those read by their teammates. This has the benefit of making the experts possessors of completely unique information, and thus makes the teams value each member's contribution more highly. For example, in a unit on Chile, one student might have information on Chile's economy, another on its geography, a third on its history. To know all about Chile, students must rely on their teammates. Original Jigsaw also takes less time than Jigsaw II; its readings are shorter, only a part of the total unit to be studied.

The most difficult part of original Jigsaw, and the reason Jigsaw II is presented first in this publication, is that each individual section must be written so that it is comprehensible by itself. Existing materials cannot be used as in Jigsaw II; books can rarely be divided neatly into sections that make any sense without the other sections. For example, in a biography of Alexander Hamilton, the section describing his duel with Aaron Burr would assume that the reader knew who both men were (having read the rest of the biography). Preparing an original Jigsaw unit involves rewriting material to fit the Jigsaw format. The added advantage of Jigsaw II is that all students read all the material, which may make unified concepts easier to understand.

Teachers who wish to use original Jigsaw to capitalize on its special features giving the experts unique information (which may contribute to Jigsaw's positive effects on student self-esteem) can use Jigsaw II with these modifications:

1. Write units that present unique information about a subject but make sense by themselves. This can be done by cutting apart texts and adding information as needed, or by writing completely new material.
2. Assign students to five- or six-member teams and make five topics for each unit.
3. Appoint team leaders and emphasize team-building exercises before and during use of the technique. Team building involves activities that help the teams learn how to work well together and get to know one another. Part of team building after the beginning is process analysis—asking members to analyze the strengths and weaknesses of their team operation.
4. Use quizzes less frequently and do not use team scores, improvement scores, or newsletters. Simply give students individual grades.

For more information on original Jigsaw, see *The Jigsaw Classroom* (Aronson et al. 1978).

Other Ways of Using Jigsaw

Jigsaw is one of the most flexible of the Student Team Learning methods. Several modifications can be made that keep the basic model but change the details of implementation.

1. Instead of having the topics refer to narrative materials given to students, have students search a set of classroom or library materials to find information on their topics.
2. Have students write essays or give oral reports instead of taking quizzes after completing the experts' reports.
3. Instead of having all teams study the same material, give each team a unique topic to learn together and each team member a subtopic. The team could then prepare and make an oral presentation to the entire class. This strategy is described in detail by Sharan and Sharan (1976).

TEAM ACCELERATED INSTRUCTION

Team Accelerated Instruction, or TAI, is not described completely in this book because it cannot be used in the classroom from a description alone (in contrast to STAD, TGT, and Jigsaw). Information on mathematics materials and teachers' manuals designed for TAI may be obtained from the Johns Hopkins Team Learning Project (see the preface for the address).

Application. TAI is designed for use in all grades two through eight mathematics classes, except junior high algebra classes.

Teams. Students are assigned to four- to five-member, heterogeneous teams as in STAD, TGT, and Jigsaw II.

Placement test. Students are pretested on mathematics operations and placed at the appropriate point in the individualized program based on their test performance.

Curriculum materials. For operations skills (addition, subtraction, multiplication, division, numeration, decimals, fractions, ratios, percent, algebra, and word problems), students work on individualized curriculum materials that have the following subparts:

1. A guide page explaining the skill to be mastered and giving a step-by-step method of solving problems.
2. Several skill pages, each consisting of 20 problems. Each skill

page introduces a subskill that leads to final mastery of the entire skill. For example, a unit on adding with renaming consists of a skill page on decoding whether or not renaming is necessary, a second skill page on adding the tens column, and a final skill page on adding the ones column, performing the renaming, and adding the tens column to get the final answer.

3. A formative test consisting of two parallel sets of 10 items.
4. A unit test.
5. Answer sheets for skill pages, formative tests, and unit tests.

Students work on these individualized units for three in every four weeks. During each fourth week, skills other than operations, such as geometry, sets, and measurement, are taught using group-paced methods. These units are not included in the individualized materials because they do not require the level of prior skills needed for the operations units; therefore they can be taught more efficiently to the entire class.

Team study method. After they take the diagnostic test, students are assigned a starting place in the individualized mathematics units. They work on their units in teams, exchanging answer sheets with partners. Students work four problems on their skill pages and then check with their partners. If all four problems are correct, they may go on to the next skill page; if not, they must work the next four problems, until four in a row are correct. If students have difficulty with the sets of four problems, they may call on a teammate or the teacher for help. When students have finished all skill pages, they may take a 10-item formative test; if they answer eight or more items correctly, they may take the unit test. One of the three student monitors selected each day scores the test.

Team scores. At the end of each week, the teacher compiles a team score. Teams receive 10 points for every unit completed by any team member, plus 2 points for each perfect paper, and 1 point for each paper with only one incorrect answer.

Team recognition. Criteria are established for team performance. Meeting a high criterion qualifies a team as a Superteam. Meeting other criteria may qualify teams as Greatteams or Goodteams. Members of such teams receive certificates.

Teaching groups. Every day the teacher works for 15 to 20 minutes with at least one group of 6 to 10 students who are at about the same point in the curriculum. The purpose of these sessions is to go over concepts, explain any points causing students trouble, and prepare students for upcoming units. During this time, other students continue working on their own units.

Curriculum organization. The curriculum is organized into 12 skills:

addition, subtraction, multiplication, division, fractions, decimals, numeration, percent, ratios, statistics, algebra, and word problems. The units in each skill area are arranged in a definite sequence in which each unit depends on mastery of the last unit.

COOPERATIVE INTEGRATED READING AND COMPOSITION

The Cooperative Integrated Reading and Composition, or CIRC, program consists of three principal elements: basal-related activities, direct instruction in reading comprehension, and integrated language arts and writing. In all these activities, students work in heterogeneous learning teams. All activities follow a regular cycle that involves teacher presentation, team practice, independent practice, peer preassessment, additional practice, and testing. As in the case for TAI, CIRC has its own manual and materials and therefore cannot be implemented from this book alone. The major components of the CIRC program are as follows:

Reading groups and teams. In CIRC, students are assigned to two or three reading groups according to their reading level, as determined by their teachers.

Students are also assigned to pairs (or triads) within their reading groups, and then the pairs are assigned to teams composed of partnerships from two reading groups. For example, a team might be composed of two students from the top reading group and two from the low group. Team members receive points based on their individual performances on all quizzes, compositions, and book reports, and these points are contributed to form a team score. Teams that meet an average criterion of 95 percent on all activities in a given week are designated Superteams; those that meet an average criterion of 90 percent are designated Greatteams; and those that meet a more moderate criterion are designated Goodteams. All receive certificates.

Basal-related activities. Students use their regular basal readers. Basal stories are introduced and discussed in teacher-led reading groups that meet for approximately 20 minutes each day. During these groups, teachers set a purpose for reading, introduce new vocabulary, review old vocabulary, discuss the story after students have read it. Presentation methods for each segment of the lesson are structured. For example, teachers use a vocabulary presentation procedure that requires a demonstration of understanding of word meaning by each individual, a review of methods of word attack, and repetitive oral reading of vocabulary to achieve fluency. Story discussions are structured to emphasize such skills as making and supporting predictions and identifying the problem in a narrative.

After stories are introduced, students are given a story packet that lays out a series of activities for them to do in their teams when they are not working with the teacher in a reading group. The sequence of activities is as follows:

- *Partner reading.* Students read the story silently and then take turns reading it aloud with their partners, alternating on each paragraph. Meanwhile the listener corrects any errors the reader may make. The teacher assesses student performance by circulating and listening in as students read to each other.

- *Story grammar and story-related writing.* Students are given questions (Treasure Hunts) related to each narrative emphasizing the grammar, the structure that underlies all narratives. Halfway through the story, they are instructed to stop reading and to identify the characters, the setting, and the problem in the story, and to predict how the problem will be resolved. At the end of the story students respond to the story as a whole and write a few paragraphs on a related topic (for example, they might be asked to write a different ending).

- *Words out loud.* Students are given a list of new or difficult words used in the story that they must be able to read correctly in any order without hesitating or stumbling. Students practice these word lists with their partners or other teammates until they can read them smoothly.

- *Word meaning.* Students are given a list of story words that are new in their speaking vocabularies and are asked to look them up in a dictionary, paraphrase the definition, and write a sentence for each that shows the meaning of the word (i.e., "An *octopus* grabbed the swimmer with its eight long legs," not "I have an *octopus*").

- *Story retell.* After reading the story and discussing it in their reading groups, students summarize the main points to their partners.

- *Spelling.* Students pretest one another on a list of spelling words each week and then work over the course of the week to help one another master the list. Students use a "disappearing list" strategy in which they make new lists of missed words after each assessment until the list disappears and they go back to the full list, repeating the process as many times as necessary.

- *Partner checking.* After students complete each of the preceding activities, their partners initial a student assignment form indicating that they have completed and/or achieved criteria on that task. Students are given daily expectations as to the number of activities to be completed, but they can go at their own rate and complete the activities earlier if they wish, creating additional time for independent reading.

- *Tests.* At the end of three class periods, students are given a comprehension test on the story, are asked to write meaningful sentences for each vocabulary word, and are asked to read the word list aloud to the teacher. Students are not permitted to help one another on these tests. The test scores and evaluations of the story-related writing are major components of students' weekly team scores.

Direct instruction in reading comprehension. One day each week, students receive direct instruction in specific reading comprehension skills (e.g., identifying main ideas, understanding causal relations, making inferences). A special step-by-step curriculum was designed for this purpose. After each lesson, students work on reading comprehension worksheets and/or games as a whole team, first gaining consensus on one set of worksheet items and then assessing one another and discussing any remaining problems on a second set of items.

Integrated language arts and writing. During language arts periods, teachers use a specific language arts and writing curriculum especially developed for CIRC. In it, students work as teams on language arts skills that lead directly to writing activities. The emphasis of this curriculum is on writing; language mechanics skills are introduced as specific aids to writing rather than as separate topics. For example, students study modifiers during a lesson on writing descriptive paragraphs, and they study quotation marks as a part of writing dialogue in the context of a narrative. The writing program uses both writers' workshops, in which students write on topics of their choice, and specific, teacher-directed writing lessons focused on such skills as writing compare/contrast paragraphs, newspaper articles, mystery stories, and letters. On all writing assignments students draft compositions after consultation about their ideas and organizational plans with their teammates and the teacher; they work with teammates to revise the content of their compositions; and then they edit one another's work using peer editing forms emphasizing grammatical and mechanical correctness. The peer editing forms begin very simply, but as students cover successive skills the forms are made increasingly complex. Finally, students "publish" their final compositions in team and/or class books.

Independent reading. Every evening, students are asked to read a trade book of their choice for at least 20 minutes. Parents initial forms indicating that students have read the required time, and students contribute points to their teams if they submit a completed form each week. Students also complete at least one book report every two weeks, for which they also receive team points. Independent reading and book reports replace all other homework in reading and language arts. If students complete their story packets or other activities early, they may also read their independent reading books in class.

OTHER COOPERATIVE LEARNING METHODS

Although the majority of teachers who use Student Team Learning in their classrooms use STAD, TGT, Jigsaw, TAI, CIRC, or some combination of these methods, many have seen the need to modify the basic techniques for particular purposes or special situations. Several extensions or modifications of

Student Team Learning have been created to meet special needs. These modifications are described in *Using Student Team Learning* (Slavin 1986), which can be obtained from the Johns Hopkins Team Learning Project (see the preface for the address).

TROUBLESHOOTING

As they use Student Team Learning, teachers may experience a few problems. Some of these problems and the solutions that other teachers have found effective are as follows.

Team members not getting along. This problem often comes up in the first week or two of use of Student Team Learning. Remember, a team is made up of the most unlikely combination possible. Students differ from one another in sex ethnicity, and academic performance level.

The primary solution for this problem is time. Some students will be unhappy about their team assignments initially, but as soon as they realize that they will be working in the teams for a long time, and especially when they receive their first team scores and realize that they really are a team and need to cooperate to be successful, they will find a way to get along. For this reason, it is important not to allow students to change teams; what makes the teammates work on their problems is the recognition that they will be together for many weeks.

Some students, however, will need constant reminding that their task is to cooperate with their teammates. It is important to set a firm tone that cooperation with teammates is appropriate behavior during team practice. No one should be forced to work with a team; individuals who refuse (this happens rarely) should be allowed to work alone until they are ready to join the team. However, it should be clear to students that putdowns, making fun of teammates, or refusing to help them are ineffective ways for teams to be successful and not acceptable kinds of behavior.

One effective way to improve student cooperation is to provide extra rewards to winning teams. Sometimes students will not care how the team or their teammates are doing until they know that the winning team will receive refreshments, time off, release from a test. Some teachers give the members of the week's winning team an automatic A grade for the week.

It is also a good idea to have students who work in pairs within their teams switch partners from time to time, to reemphasize the need for team effort not just individual preparation.

If some teams do not work out, the teacher may decide to change teams after three or four weeks instead of six, reassigning students in ways that avoid the problems encountered in the first team assignments.

Misbehavior. One way to encourage students to behave appropriately is to give each team up to three additional team points each day based on the team's behavior, cooperativeness, and effort. In such cases, it is also important that the teacher move from team to team telling them what they are doing right (for example, "I see the Cougars working well together.... The Fantastic Four are all in their seats and doing their work.... The Chiefs are working quietly...."). The points earned for team behavior should definitely not be a surprise, but should reflect teacher comments during the period.

Noise. Noise is more of a problem in some schools than others, depending on acoustics, open versus traditional construction, and school attitudes toward noise. Student Team Learning does not go well with the teacher shushing students every five minutes, but if things are so noisy that students cannot hear each other, something should be done.

The first solution to try for the noise problem is to bring all activity to a stop, get absolute quiet, and then whisper a reminder to students to speak softly. Students should be taught to stop talking immediately when the lights are flicked off for a moment, or a bell sounds, or some other signal is given. If this does not work, try to make noise level part of the criteria for earning extra team points just noted.

If students can hear each other and not get out of hand, try to learn to tolerate their on-task noise if possible.

Absences. Student absenteeism can be a major problem in a Student Team Learning class because students depend on one another to contribute points to the team. The solution, however, is relatively simple in classrooms where absenteeism is not extremely high. When students miss a tournament or a quiz, prorate the scores for their teams that week, using Appendix A (in Chapter 4). For example, if one student on a four-member team was absent for the tournament or quiz, prorate that team's score as for a three-member team.

When Student Team Learning is to be used in a class with very poor attendance, poor attenders should be distributed evenly among teams as fifth or sixth members, so that at least three or four students will be likely to show up on each team each day. If there are some students who never or almost never attend, they may be left out of the team system and reincluded if they start coming to class more regularly.

Ineffective use of team practice time. If students do not use their time in team practice effectively, the teacher can impose some kind of structure on the team practice sessions to be sure that they use the time well.

One problem is that students may be used to doing their worksheets alone and thinking they are finished when they reach the end, whether or not they or their teammates understand the material. This problem is dealt with primarily by providing only two worksheets per team so that students have to work together. Teachers can also make (or have students make) flashcards with questions on one side and answers on the other, and have students drill each other in pairs or threes, putting correctly answered items in one pile and missed items in another. Students go through the missed pile until they have correctly answered everything once, and then go through the entire set again until each student can achieve 100% on the items in any order. This will work only if the answers are short. If the answers require figuring, as in most of mathematics, then students should work in pairs or threes, going through the items one at a time and checking answers after everyone has finished each item. If anyone missed a question, any teammates who answered it correctly should explain what they did. In either of these cases, students should change partners within their teams every 30 minutes or so, to make sure that teammates do not form little subteams.

Performance level range too wide for group instruction. If teachers have this problem, it is first important to think about what they were doing before using Student Team Learning. Those who were using whole-group instruction can use Student Team Learning, but they need to take time to work with low performers to help get them up to the level of the rest of the class. Teachers of grades two through eight should use TAI or CIRC if they can obtain these materials because these programs accommodate instruction to individual needs and can solve the problem of a wide performance range.

Problems with the TGT tournament. Usually there are few tournament problems that cannot be handled by simply making a rules interpretation. The problems that arise often come from a misreading of the rules or of the manual. For example, some teachers do not allow students to reshuffle the cards at the end of one game and go through the deck again. Many teachers complain that students at the higher tables do not want to play the game again, so they provide extra resource material for those students to work with. Nevertheless, if at all possible, encourage students to play two or more games if they finish theirs first. Make sure, however, that although game scores are recorded after each game, tournament points are computed only once, at the end of the period; the maximum tournament points a player may earn is always 6, no matter how many games are played. Although students should be allowed to play the game more than once, the teacher should call time when it is obvious that the entire class has gone through the cards at least once and is not eager to continue.

Another frequent misreading of the TGT game rules involves challenges. If a student challenges and is wrong, he or she returns a previously won card (if any) to the deck. Students never give each other cards they have won previously.

At times players complain that certain students had more chances than others to earn points because of their starting positions. This is a serious problem when some tables are getting 90 to 100 percent of the items correct, and one extra turn may determine the winner. To create a totally fair competition, first be sure that the number of items is a multiple of the number of players (for example, 30 items for three players). For four-person tournament tables, simply remove two number cards from the deck to get the correct multiple (for example, 28 items for four players). Thus, for any table where all items are answered correctly, players will have an equal chance to win. When you call time to end the tournament, let any tables where all players have not had an equal number of turns continue to play until everyone has had the same number of turns.

Occasionally a teacher will have some students who just cannot handle the competition. If this is a widespread problem, switch to STAD. If it is a problem for only a few students, withdraw a student from the competition, give him or her the game sheet as a quiz, and grade the quiz on a scale of 2 to 6 to correspond to a TGT score.

Problems with STAD. Almost all problems with STAD are problems with teams, discussed earlier. However, STAD has one additional problem. Because of the use of the individual improvement score system, some previously high-performing students (and occasionally their parents) complain that it is not fair that they have to do so much better to get the same points as a low-performing student. To answer this concern, emphasize the following:

1. The individual improvement score system is fair because in order to earn maximum points, everyone has to show improvement each week, not just perform at the same level as before. Improving by 10 points is just as hard for a low-performing student as it is for a high-performing student.
2. Because a maximum of 10 points is possible, and because a perfect paper is always worth 10 points, no student with a low base score can earn a higher number of points than one with the best possible quiz score.
3. Although team points are based on improvement, grades are still determined in the usual way. Thus, high-performing students who continue to perform at a high level will still receive high grades.

Another problem that arises with STAD is that occasionally, because a particular quiz is very difficult, almost everyone will get zero points. When this happens, give each item $1^1/_2$ or 2 points because it is unfair to penalize the entire class if the test is too difficult. If large numbers of students keep performing below their base scores, the material being taught is probably above the level of the class, and either the pace should be slowed or more appropriate material chosen.

Problems with Jigsaw. Team presentations in Jigsaw are so structured that little can go wrong with them, except that students should be held to a firm time limit for each presentation in order not to take up too much class time.

The expert groups are much less concretely structured and thus more prone to problems. When students do not seem to be using their expert group time well, the general solution is to provide more structure.

Some teachers provide a set of discussion topics for expert groups and have the expert group leader call on students to contribute to each discussion.

Another way to make the expert groups more effective is to have an aide, parent, or older student act as discussion leader. Also, the teacher may be able to stagger the schedule of expert groups so that she or he can work with each group. Most expert groups do not need this kind of help, but when students are either young or lack self-organization skills, they need some additional structure.

Absenteeism is a special problem in Jigsaw because it is important for every team to have an expert on every topic. One way to deal with very serious absenteeism is to make six-member teams and have students work on each of three topics in pairs, so that at least one student is likely to appear for each topic. Another solution is to make the readings very short, so that students can read, discuss their topics in their expert groups, and take their quizzes all in the same period. Or reduce the number of topics to three—at least three students are likely to be present to take the topics, and this averts the problem of absent team members.

Scoring problems. Teachers often find several things about scoring difficult or confusing.

Bumping in TGT is not usually a serious problem, except that teachers need to be prepared to reassign students when someone assigned to a particular tournament table is absent. Also, new students should not automatically be assigned to the bottom of the bumping scheme. This gives them a considerable advantage until they are bumped up to the proper table. New students should be assigned to tables on the basis of some test or past grade.

Team scores also present few problems. Some teachers forget to prorate for teams larger or smaller than four members. This gives teams an unfair advantage or disadvantage; prorating is very important.

The individual improvement score system used in STAD and Jigsaw II is not very difficult, but mistakes are sometimes made. It is essential to remember that the maximum improvement score is 10 and that perfect quizzes get 10 points regardless of the base score. It is also essential to readjust base scores every two weeks. Not doing so is a serious problem, because a student whose base score was set too low or too high and is not changed has an unfair advantage or disadvantage. Some teachers give students zeros for skipping class or for some disciplinary problem. Give students zero improvement points toward their team score if they skip class, but never count these scores as zeros in refiguring base scores; consider them blank for that purpose.

Too much work for teachers. "Too much work" is the most frequently heard complaint about Student Team Learning from teachers, especially from those who are making their own materials. However, there are some ways to reduce the work required.

One way is to have students help with the scoring and newsletter writing. Responsibility for writing the newsletter can be passed from team to team, and volunteer students can come in after school to help score quizzes, calculate team scores, or do the bumping for TGT. Scoring quizzes is the biggest job in terms of teacher time, but it is also the easiest to get help with; students can either exchange papers in class or entire classes can exchange papers. Volunteer students can also make ditto masters and run off materials.

For teachers using the Johns Hopkins Team Learning Project materials, additional curriculum material is not difficult to make. However, it is a bigger job for those who are making materials from scratch. In such cases, the best arrangement is for teachers in the same department or grade level to cooperate in making a set of materials, with each teacher taking responsibility for part of the curriculum. The result will be a central library of curriculum materials that all teachers can use. Existing worksheets and quizzes from previous years can also be incorporated into this library, and whenever teachers add a unit, it, too, can be made available for colleagues to use.

APPENDIX A:
Prorating Scores for Teams with Two, Three, or Five Members

Raw Scores	Five-Member Team	Three-Member Team	Two-Member Team
4			8
5			10
6		8	12
7		9	14
8		11	16
9		12	18
10	8	13	20
11	9	15	22
12	10	16	24
13	11	17	26
14	12	19	28
15	12	20	30
16	13	21	32
17	14	23	34
18	14	24	36
19	15	25	38
20	16	27	40
21	17	28	
22	18	29	
23	18	31	
24	19	32	
25	20	33	
26	21	35	
27	22	36	
28	22	37	
29	23	39	
30	24	40	
31	25		
32	26		
33	26		
34	27		
35	28		
36	29		
37	30		
38	30		
39	31		
40	32		
41	33		
42	35		
43	34		
44	35		
45	36		
46	37		
47	38		
48	38		
49	39		
50	40		

APPENDIX B:
Calculating New Base Scores

To find the new base score, add the student's two quiz scores together, and find the total in the column to the left. Find the student's old base score at the top. Follow the row across and the column down until you come to where they intersect. This number is the student's new base score.

Total of Quiz Scores	Old Base Score										
	3	4	5	6	7	8	9	10	11	12	13
16	3	3	4	4	4	5	5	5	6	6	6
17	3	4	4	4	5	5	5	6	6	6	7
18	4	4	4	5	5	5	6	6	6	7	7
19	4	4	5	5	5	6	6	6	7	7	7
20	4	5	5	5	6	6	6	7	7	7	8
21	5	5	5	6	6	6	7	7	7	8	8
22	5	5	6	6	6	7	7	7	8	8	8
23	5	6	6	6	7	7	7	8	8	8	9
24	6	6	6	7	7	7	8	8	8	9	9
25	6	6	7	7	7	8	8	8	9	9	9
26	6	7	7	7	8	8	8	9	9	9	10
27	7	7	7	8	8	8	9	9	9	10	10
28	7	7	8	8	8	9	9	9	10	10	10
29	7	8	8	8	9	9	9	10	10	10	11
30	8	8	8	9	9	9	10	10	10	11	11
31	8	8	9	9	9	10	10	10	11	11	11
32	8	9	9	9	10	10	10	11	11	11	12
33	9	9	9	10	10	10	11	11	11	12	12
34	9	9	10	10	10	11	11	11	12	12	12
35	9	10	10	10	11	11	11	12	12	12	13
36	10	10	10	11	11	11	12	12	12	13	13
37	10	10	11	11	11	12	12	12	13	13	13
38	10	11	11	11	12	12	12	13	13	13	14
39	11	11	11	12	12	12	13	13	13	14	14
40	11	11	12	12	12	13	13	13	14	14	14
41	11	12	12	12	13	13	13	14	14	14	15
42	12	12	12	13	13	13	14	14	14	15	15
43	12	12	13	13	13	14	14	14	15	15	15
44	12	13	13	13	14	14	14	15	15	15	16
45	13	13	13	14	14	14	15	15	15	16	16
46	13	13	14	14	14	15	15	15	16	16	16
47	13	14	14	14	15	15	15	16	16	16	17
48	14	14	14	15	15	15	16	16	16	17	17
49	14	14	15	15	15	16	16	16	17	17	17
50	14	15	15	15	16	16	16	17	17	17	18
51	15	15	15	16	16	16	17	17	17	18	18
52	15	15	16	16	16	17	17	17	18	18	18
53	15	16	16	16	17	17	17	18	18	18	19
54	16	16	16	17	17	17	18	18	18	19	19
55	16	16	17	17	17	18	18	18	19	19	19
56	16	17	17	17	18	18	18	19	19	19	20
57	17	17	17	18	18	18	19	19	19	20	20
58	17	17	18	18	18	19	19	19	20	20	20
59	17	18	18	18	19	19	19	20	20	20	21
60	18	18	18	19	19	19	20	20	20	21	21

Total of Quiz Scores	Old Base Score											
	14	15	16	17	18	19	20	21	22	23	24	25
16	7	7	7	8	8	8	9	9	9	10	10	10
17	7	7	8	8	8	9	9	9	10	10	10	11
18	7	8	8	8	9	9	9	10	10	10	11	11
19	8	8	8	9	9	9	10	10	10	11	11	11
20	8	8	9	9	9	10	10	10	11	11	11	12
21	8	9	9	9	10	10	10	11	11	11	12	12
22	9	9	9	10	10	10	11	11	11	12	12	12
23	9	9	10	10	10	11	11	11	12	12	12	13
24	9	10	10	10	11	11	11	12	12	12	13	13
25	10	10	10	11	11	11	12	12	12	13	13	13
26	10	10	11	11	11	12	12	12	13	13	13	14
27	10	11	11	11	12	12	12	13	13	13	14	14
28	11	11	11	12	12	12	13	13	13	14	14	14
29	11	11	12	12	12	13	13	13	14	14	14	15
30	11	12	12	12	13	13	13	14	14	14	15	15
31	12	12	12	13	13	13	14	14	14	15	15	15
32	12	12	13	13	13	14	14	14	15	15	15	16
33	12	12	13	13	14	14	14	15	15	15	16	16
34	13	13	13	14	14	14	15	15	15	16	16	16
35	13	13	14	14	14	15	15	15	16	16	16	17
36	13	14	14	14	15	15	15	16	16	16	17	17
37	14	14	14	15	15	15	16	16	16	17	17	17
38	14	14	15	15	15	16	16	16	17	17	17	18
39	14	15	15	15	16	16	16	17	17	17	18	18
40	15	15	15	16	16	16	17	17	17	18	18	18
41	15	15	16	16	16	17	17	17	18	18	18	19
42	15	16	16	16	17	17	17	18	18	18	19	19
43	16	16	16	17	17	17	18	18	18	19	19	19
44	16	16	17	17	17	18	18	18	19	19	19	20
45	16	17	17	17	18	18	18	19	19	19	20	20
46	17	17	17	18	18	18	19	19	19	20	20	20
47	17	17	18	18	18	19	19	19	20	20	20	21
48	17	18	18	18	19	19	19	20	20	20	21	21
49	18	18	18	19	19	19	20	20	20	21	21	21
50	18	18	19	19	19	20	20	20	21	21	21	22
51	18	19	19	19	20	20	20	21	21	21	22	22
52	19	19	19	20	20	20	21	21	21	22	22	22
53	19	19	20	20	20	21	21	21	22	22	22	23
54	19	20	20	20	21	21	21	22	22	22	23	23
55	20	20	20	21	21	21	22	22	22	23	23	23
56	20	20	21	21	21	22	22	22	23	23	23	24
57	20	21	21	21	22	22	22	23	23	23	24	24
58	21	21	21	22	22	22	23	23	23	24	24	24
59	21	21	22	22	22	23	23	23	24	24	24	25
60	21	22	22	22	23	23	23	24	24	24	25	25

APPENDIX C:
Instructions for Making Worksheets and Games/Quizzes for STAD and TGT, with Samples

Making curriculum materials for Student Teams-Achievement Divisions or Teams-Games-Tournament is very much like making worksheets and quizzes you already have, or you may take items from other sources instead of creating entirely new worksheets and quizzes.

To make materials for STAD or TGT, follow these steps:

1. Make a worksheet and a worksheet answer sheet for each unit. A worksheet is usually a series of items that provides students with practice and self-assessment that will directly help them prepare for the quiz (STAD) or game (TGT) to follow. The number of worksheet items depends on the kind of material you are teaching. Short-answer items, such as irregular verb tenses, multiplication facts, or multiple-choice questions, probably require a longer worksheet than a unit in which each item takes longer to do, as in a long division unit. The Johns Hopkins Team Learning Project curriculum materials always use 30-item worksheets and the individual improvement score system is based on 30-item quizzes. Thus, although it is not necessary to make that exact number of items, it is best to include in the quizzes a total number of items that divide into 30 evenly, such as 5, 10, or 15.

A set of items is not the only possible kind of worksheet. For example, in a geography unit students can fill in country names on a blank map, and in a math facts or spelling unit they can use flashcards instead of a worksheet. The main idea is to be sure that the worksheet provides *direct* practice for the quiz or game. For example, a crossword puzzle may give students some help with a spelling test, but it does not give them the kind of drill and practice that will enable them to master the spelling words. Thus, a crossword puzzle can be used as a supplementary activity, but it should not be used to replace a worksheet or flash cards that directly prepare students for a spelling test.

As soon as you have made a worksheet, also make a worksheet answer sheet. Students will use this answer sheet to check themselves as they study.

2. Make a game/quiz and a game/quiz answer sheet for each unit. The same sheet serves as a game in TGT and a quiz in STAD. The items on this sheet should closely parallel those on the worksheet. Develop the worksheet and the game/quiz at the same time, making each worksheet item parallel to each corresponding game/quiz item. The following are examples of parallel items:

70

Worksheet	Game/Quiz
1. ½ + ½ =	1. 1/3 + 1/3 =
2. The car crept _____ up the hill.	2. Even though he was nervous, he got a
a. slow	_____ score on the test.
b. slowly	a. good
3. A combination of hydrogen and flourine	b. well
would be written . . .	3. A combination of calcium and chlorine
a. H_2F	would be written . . .
b. HF	a. Ca_2Cl
c. HF_2	b. CaCl
d. H_2F_2	c. $CaCl_2$
4. The capital of Canada is _____.	d. Ca_2Cl_2
	4. The capital of Canada is _____.

Note that in questions 1 to 3, the parallel items test the same skill or concept (addition of simple fractions with like denominators, correct use of adjectives/adverbs, writing chemical formulas with elements of different valences), but they are different items. This avoids the possibility of students memorizing the *items* instead of learning the *concepts*. In item 4, however, the task is to memorize capitals of countries. Thus it is appropriate to give the same item twice, and it would of course be unfair to have a capital on the game/quiz that did not appear on the worksheet.

The number of items on the game/quiz should ordinarily be 30. This corresponds to the number of cards used in TGT or to the number used as the basis of the individual improvement score system in STAD. However, you may use shorter or longer games/quizzes if you wish. For TGT, to use any number of items up to 30, have students remove number cards for which there are no items. For STAD, use quizzes with a number of items that divides evenly into 30. For example, for a 15-item quiz, give two points for each correct answer.

For TGT, you will need to make a game/quiz answer sheet so that students can check themselves during the game. For STAD, you will need a correction key. If students correct each other's papers, you can place the answers on an overhead projector sheet or on a large piece of paper to show the class, or simply read the answers to students for correction.

A representative unit, consisting of a worksheet, worksheet answers, game/quiz, and game/quiz answers, follows.

Student Team Learning

Subject: Mathematics

Worksheet: R-7   Subtraction of Three Digit Numbers

Topics: - subtracting three digits with renaming
         - word problems

Subtract

1. 574
  - 297
	6. 666
	  - 148
		11. 804
		  - 425
			16. 249
			  - 168

2. 847
  - 658
	7. 743
	  - 267
		12. 628
		  - 447
			17. 463
			  - 276

3. 902
  - 627
	8. 426
	  - 148
		13. 507
		  - 318
			18. 912
			  - 655

4. 733
  - 286
	9. 525
	  - 437
		14. 624
		  - 368
			19. 647
			  - 152

5. 655
  - 257
	10. 917
	  - 648
		15. 501
		  - 287
			20. 431
			  - 265

Worksheet: R-7 Subtraction of Three Digit Numbers

Subject: Mathematics

21. 723
   - 546

22. 823
   - 568

23. 814
   - 657

24. 734
   - 376

25. 642
   - 286

Solve the word problems.

26. There are 990 coins on the table. Bob takes 648 of them. How many coins are left?

27. There are 502 balloons. 249 of them are blue. How many balloons are not blue?

28. In a box there are 308 apples. Jane takes 198 of them. How many apples are left in the box?

29. There are 503 children in the school. There are 246 boys. How many girls are there?

30. There are 432 crayons. Jackie broke 243 of them. How many crayons are unbroken?

Worksheet Answers
Subject: Mathematics

R-7 Subtraction of Three Digit Numbers

1.	277	16.	81
2.	189	17.	187
3.	275	18.	257
4.	447	19.	495
5.	398	20.	166
6.	518	21.	177
7.	476	22.	255
8.	278	23.	157
9.	88	24.	358
10.	269	25.	356
11.	379	26.	342 coins
12.	181	27.	253 balloons
13.	189	28.	110 apples
14.	256	29.	257 girls
15.	214	30.	189 crayons

Student Team Learning

Subject: Mathematics

Game/Quiz: R-7   Subtraction of Three Digit Numbers

Subtract

1. 735
   - 278
	6. 777
	   - 188
		11. 404
		    - 116
			16. 307
			    - 75

2. 465
   - 386
	7. 734
	   - 376
		12. 737
		    - 609
			17. 724
			    - 567

3. 957
   - 648
	8. 516
	   - 245
		13. 402
		    - 138
			18. 624
			    - 395

4. 803
   - 627
	9. 626
	   - 447
		14. 456
		    - 398
			19. 647
			    - 152

5. 655
   - 347
	10. 818
	    - 520
		15. 812
		    - 566
			20. 431
			    - 265

Subject: Mathematics

21.	515 - 369	22.	991 - 709	23.	502 - 369	24.	423 - 245

25.   872
    - 516

Solve the word problems

26. There are 112 balls in the gym. 88 are flat. How many ball are not flat?

27. There are 409 pencils. 22 are red pencils. How many pencils are not red?

28. Jim has 931 candy bars. He gives away 646 of them. How many candy bars does he keep?

29. There are 871 doors in the hotel. 575 are closed. How many doors are open?

30. There are 1000 papers on the floors. Jack picks up 827 of them. How many papers are still on the floor?

Game/Quiz Answers

Subject: Mathematics

R-7   Subtraction of Three Digit Numbers

1.	457	16.	232	
2.	79	17.	157	
3.	309	18.	229	
4.	176	19.	495	
5.	308	20.	166	
6.	589	21.	146	
7.	358	22.	282	
8.	271	23.	133	
9.	179	24.	178	
10.	298	25.	356	
11.	288	26.	24 balls	
12.	128	27.	387 pencils	
13.	264	28.	285 candy bars	
14.	58	29.	296 doors	
15.	246	30.	173 papers	

APPENDIX D:
Sample Jigsaw II Unit

This appendix contains an example of an Expert Sheet and a quiz—the materials needed in addition to the reading selection for a complete Jigsaw II unit. The Expert Sheet and quiz included here are based on Chapters 1 and 2 in this publication.

You might use this sample unit with other teachers to get a student's-eye view of the technique before using Jigsaw II. Assign yourself to a team, pick one of the four topics on the sample Expert Sheet, and reread Chapter 1 and 2. Then discuss the topic with your expert group, return to your team to report on your topic, and take the quiz. (The quiz answers are c, b, a, b, a, c, d, d.)

Sample Expert Sheet: Student Team Learning

Read: Chapters 1 and 2 in this publication

Topics: 1. What are the principal features of STAD, TGT, and Jigsaw?
2. What has the research on Student Team Learning found?
3. Why do the Student Team Learning Techniques produce the effects that they do?
4. What are some of the reasons that teachers might adopt one of the Student Team Learning techniques?

Sample Quiz: Student Team Learning

1a. What is the main difference between STAD and TGT?
   a. STAD is less expensive to use than TGT.
   b. STAD is used mostly in social studies, TGT in mathematics and language arts.
   c. STAD uses quizzes, TGT uses instructional games.
   d. STAD uses practice worksheets, TGT does not.

1b. What do TGT and Jigsaw have in common?
   a. Expert groups
   b. Heterogeneous teams
   c. Quizzes
   d. Instructional games

2a. Which of the Student Team Learning techniques has been evaluated in the largest number of studies?
   a. TGT

b. STAD

c. Jigsaw

2b. Which of the following is the most consistent finding for all Student Team Learning techniques?

a. Improved attitudes

b. Improved intergroup relations

c. Increased self-esteem

d. Increased satisfaction

3a. Which of the following is a reason implied in Chapters 1 and 2 for the effects of team techniques on learning?

a. Peer support for academic performance

b. Effectiveness of peer tutoring

c. Increased mutual concern

d. Improved student attitudes

3b. Which is *not* a reason implied in Chapters 1 and 2 for the effects of Student Team Learning on positive intergroup relations?

a. Students in multiethnic teams must interact.

b. Teams in general increase mutual concerns among teammates.

c. Students in multiethnic teams learn about each other's cultures.

d. Students in multiethnic teams learn to help each other.

4a. Which is *not* a reason that a teacher might adopt Student Team Learning techniques?

a. Team techniques allow the teacher to be a facilitator rather than a director.

b. Team techniques improve student learning, positive intergroup relations, and other dimensions.

c. Team techniques provide an effective classroom management system.

d. Team techniques take less time than traditional techniques.

4b. Which traditional classroom activity do STAD and TGT replace most effectively?

a. Teacher lectures

b. Supplementary activities

c. Homework

d. Drill

APPENDIX E:
Sample Record Forms

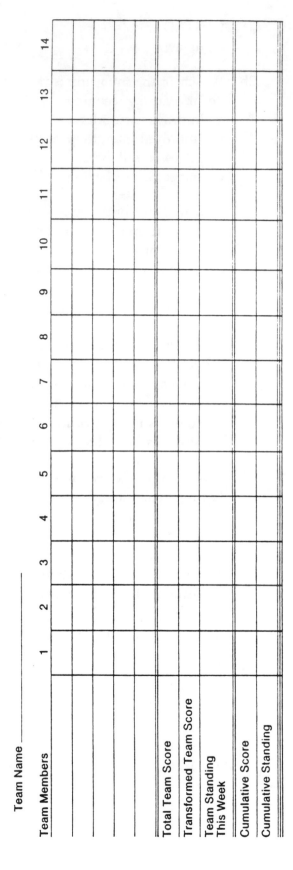

TEAM SUMMARY SHEET

Team Name _____

Team Members	1	2	3	4	5	6	7	8	9	10	11	12	13	14
Total Team Score														
Transformed Team Score														
Team Standing This Week														
Cumulative Score														
Cumulative Standing														

80

QUIZ SCORE SHEET (STAD and Jigsaw II)

| Student | Date: | | | Date: | | | Date: | | |
| | Quiz: | | | Quiz: | | | Quiz: | | |
	Base Score	Quiz Score	Improvement Points	Base Score	Quiz Score	Improvement Points	Base Score	Quiz Score	Improvement Points

TOURNAMENT TABLE ASSIGNMENT SHEET (TGT)

Tournament Number:

Student	Team	1	2	3	4	5	6	7	8	9	10	11	12	13

TABLE #_____   GAME SCORE SHEET (TGT)   ROUND #_____

PLAYER	TEAM	Game 1	Game 2	Game 3	DAY'S TOTAL	TOURNAMENT POINTS

TABLE #_____   GAME SCORE SHEET (TGT)   ROUND #_____

PLAYER	TEAM	Game 1	Game 2	Game 3	DAY'S TOTAL	TOURNAMENT POINTS

TABLE #_____   GAME SCORE SHEET (TGT)   ROUND #_____

PLAYER	TEAM	Game 1	Game 2	Game 3	DAY'S TOTAL	TOURNAMENT POINTS

TABLE #_____   GAME SCORE SHEET (TGT)   ROUND #_____

PLAYER	TEAM	Game 1	Game 2	Game 3	DAY'S TOTAL	TOURNAMENT POINTS

PART TWO

Student Team/Cooperative Learning: Views and Research

5. HERE TO STAY—OR GONE TOMORROW?

by Robert E. Slavin

Cooperative learning seems to be an extraordinary success. It has an excellent research base, many viable and successful forms, and hundreds of thousands of enthusiastic adherents. Yet every innovation in education carries within it the seeds of its own downfall, and cooperative learning is no different in this regard.

One danger inherent in the widespread adoption of cooperative learning is that large numbers of teachers with half-knowledge may use ineffective forms of the approach and experience failure and frustration. Cooperative learning appeals particularly to humanistic teachers who feel uncomfortable with a great deal of structure and with providing rewards or other "extrinsic" incentives to students. Yet research consistently finds that the successful forms of cooperative learning are those that provide a good deal of structure as well as rewards or recognition based on group performance.

At worst, some teachers hear about cooperative learning and believe that students can simply be placed in groups, given some interesting materials or problems to solve, and allowed to discover information or skills. Others may allow groups to work together to produce a single product or solution. Research clearly does not support either of these uses of the approach. Successful models always include plain old good instruction; the cooperative activities supplement but do not replace direct instruction (what they do replace is individual seatwork). Moreover, they always include individual accountability, in that group success depends on the sum of all group members' quiz scores or particular contributions to a team task.

Another danger inherent in the success of cooperative learning is that the methods will be oversold and [that teachers will be] undertrained. It is being promoted as an alternative to tracking and within-class grouping, as a means of mainstreaming academically handicapped students, as a means of improving race relations in desegregated schools, as a solution to the problems of students at risk, as a means of increasing prosocial behavior among children, as well as a method for simply increasing the achievement of all students. Cooperative learning can in fact accomplish this staggering array of objectives, but not as a result of a single three-hour inservice session.

This chapter is a guest editorial that appeared in the December 1989/January 1990 *Educational Leadership* 47 (4): 3. Reprinted with permission of the Association for Supervision and Curriculum Development. Copyright 1989 by the Association for Supervision and Curriculum Development. All rights reserved.

Real and lasting success with the approach requires in-class follow-up over time from peer coaches or expert coaches, unambiguous administrative support, and the availability of materials designed for cooperative learning or time to adapt existing materials to this purpose. It also requires using the right methods for the right objectives. For example, Student Teams-Achievement Divisions (STAD) and Teams-Games-Tournaments (TGT) are excellent for teaching skills or objectives with one right answer, from calculus to spelling to geography (Slavin 1986). I'm often depressed, however, to see these methods applied to subjects that lend themselves more to discussion and controversy.

The future of cooperative learning is difficult to predict. My hope is that even when cooperative learning is no longer the "hot" new method, schools and teachers will continue to use it as a routine part of instruction. My fear is that cooperative learning will largely disappear as a result of the faddism so common in American education.

However, I have several reasons to believe that cooperative learning is here to stay. First, it has a vastly better research base than most innovations, so it is likely to be found successful when school districts evaluate it. Second, the nature of cooperative learning makes it a method unlikely to be forced on unwilling teachers. Making mandatory such methods as mastery learning and Madeline Hunter's models, for example, has probably undermined the longevity of these methods. Third, cooperative learning appears to be becoming a standard element of preservice education, so a generation of teachers is likely to have been exposed to the idea. Finally, cooperative learning makes life more pleasant for teachers as well as for students. Students love to work together, and their enthusiasm makes teaching more fun. Long after something else is the novelty, teachers will continue to use cooperative methods because they can see the effects with their own eyes.

6. SYNTHESIS OF RESEARCH
ON COOPERATIVE LEARNING

by Robert E. Slavin

There was once a time when it was taken for granted that a quiet class was a learning class, when principals walked down the hall expecting to be able to hear a pin drop. Today, however, many schools are using programs that foster the hum of voices in classrooms. These programs, called *cooperative learning*, encourage students to discuss, debate, disagree, and ultimately to teach one another.

Cooperative learning has been suggested as the solution for an astonishing array of educational problems: it is often cited as a means of emphasizing thinking skills and increasing higher-order learning; as an alternative to ability grouping, remediation, or special education; as a means of improving race relations and acceptance of mainstreamed students; and as a way to prepare students for an increasingly collaborative work force. How many of these claims are justified? What effects do the various cooperative learning methods have on student achievement and other outcomes? Which forms of cooperative learning are most effective, and what components must be in place for cooperative learning to work?

To answer these questions, I have synthesized in this article the findings of studies of cooperative learning in elementary and secondary schools that have compared cooperative learning to traditionally taught control groups studying the same objectives over a period of at least four weeks (and up to a full school year or more). Here I present a brief summary of the effects of cooperative learning on achievement and noncognitive outcomes; for a more extensive review, see *Cooperative Learning: Theory, Research, and Practice* (Slavin 1990c).

COOPERATIVE LEARNING METHODS

There are many quite different forms of cooperative learning, but all of them involve having students work in small groups or teams to help one another learn academic material. Cooperative learning usually supplements the teacher's instruction by giving students an opportunity to discuss information or practice skills originally presented by the teacher; sometimes cooperative methods require students to find or discover information on their own. Cooperative

This chapter is an article that appeared in the February 1991 *Educational Leadership* 48 (5): 71-82. Reprinted with permission of the Association for Supervision and Curriculum Development. Copyright 1991 by the Association for Supervision and Curriculum Development. All rights reserved.

learning has been used—and investigated—in every imaginable subject in grades two to twelve and is increasingly used in college.

Small-scale laboratory research on cooperation dates back to the 1920s (see Deutch 1949; Slavin 1977c); research on specific applications of cooperative learning to the classroom began in the early 1970s. At that time, four research groups, one in Israel and three in the United states, began independently to develop and study cooperative learning methods in classroom settings.

Now researchers all over the world are studying practical applications of cooperative learning principles, and many cooperative learning principles, and many cooperative learning methods have been evaluated in one or more experimental/control comparisons. The best evaluated of the cooperative models are described below (adapted from Slavin 1990c). These include four Student Team Learning variations, Jigsaw, Learning Together, and Group Investigation.

Student Team Learning

Student Team Learning (STL) techniques were developed and researched at Johns Hopkins University. More than half of all experimental studies of practical cooperative learning methods involve STL methods.

All cooperative learning methods share the idea that students work together to learn and are responsible for one another's learning as well as their own. STL methods, in addition to this idea, emphasize the use of team goals and team success, which can only be achieved if all members of the team learn the objectives being taught. That is, in Student Team Learning the students' task are not to *do* something as a team but to *learn* something as a team.

Three concepts are central to all Student Team Learning methods: *team rewards, individual accountability,* and *equal opportunities for success.* Using STL techniques, teams earn certificates or other team rewards if they achieve above a designated criterion. The teams are not in competition to earn scarce rewards; all (or none) of the teams may achieve the criterion in a given week. *Individual accountability* means that the team's success depends on the individual learning of all team members. This focuses the activity of the team members on explaining concepts to one another and making sure that everyone on the team is ready for a quiz or other assessment that they will take without teammate help. *Equal opportunities for success* means that students contribute to their teams by improving over their own past performances. This ensures that high, average, and low achievers are equally challenged to do their best and that the contributions of all team members will be valued.

The findings of these experimental studies (summarized in this section) indicate that team rewards and individual accountability are essential elements for producing basic skills achievement (Slavin 1983a, 1983b, 1990c). It is not enough to simply tell students to work together. They must have a reason to take one another's achievement seriously. Further, if students are rewarded for doing better than they have in the past, they will be more motivated to achieve than if they are rewarded based on their performance in comparison to others, because rewards for improvement make success neither too difficult nor too easy for students to achieve (Slavin 1980).

Four principal Student Team Learning methods have been extensively developed and researched. Two are general cooperative learning methods adaptable to most subjects and grade levels: Student Teams-Achievement Divisions (STAD) and Teams-Games-Tournament (TGT). The remaining two are comprehensive curriculums designed for use in particular subjects at particular grade levels: Team Assisted Individualization (TAI) for mathematics in grades three to six and Cooperative Integrated Reading and Composition (CIRC) for reading and writing instruction in grades three to five.

Student Teams-Achievement Divisions (STAD)

In STAD (Slavin 1978, 1986), students are assigned to four-member learning teams mixed in performance level, sex, and ethnicity. The teacher presents a lesson, and then students work within their teams to make sure that all team members have mastered the lesson. Finally, all students take individual quizzes on the material, at which time they may *not* help one another.

Students' quiz scores are compared to their own past averages, and points are awarded based on the degree to which students can meet or exceed their own earlier performances. These points are then summed to form team scores, and teams that meet certain criteria earn certificates or other rewards. The whole cycle of activities, from teacher presentation to team practice to quiz, usually takes three to five class periods.

STAD have been used in a wide variety of subjects, from mathematics to language arts and social studies. They have been used from grade two through college. STAD are most appropriate for teaching well-defined objectives with single right answers, such as mathematical computations and applications, language usage and mechanics, geography and map skills, and science facts and concepts.

Teams-Games-Tournament (TGT)

Teams-Games-Tournament (DeVries and Slavin 1978; Slavin 1986) was the first of the Johns Hopkins cooperative learning methods. It uses the same teacher presentations and teamwork as in STAD, but replaces the quizzes with weekly tournaments. In these students compete with members of other teams to contribute points to their team scores. Students compete at three-person "tournament tables" against others with similar past records in mathematics. A "bumping" procedure changes table assignments to keep the competition fair. The winner at each tournament table brings the same number of points to his or her team, regardless of which table it is; this means that low achievers (competing with other low achievers) and high achievers (competing with other high achievers) have equal opportunities for success. As in STAD, high-performing teams earn certificates or other forms of team rewards. TGT is appropriate for the same types of objectives as STAD.

Team Assisted Individualization (TAI)

Team Assisted Individualization (TAI; Slavin, Leavy, and Madden 1986) shares with STAD and TGT the use of four-member mixed ability learning teams and certificates for high-performing teams. But where STAD and TGT use a single pace of instruction for the class, TAI combines cooperative learning with individualized instruction. Also, where STAD and TGT apply to most subjects and grade levels, TAI is specifically designed to teach mathematics to students in grades three to six (or older students not ready for a full algebra course).

In TAI, students enter an individualized sequence according to a placement test and then proceed at their own rates. In general, team members work on different units. Teammates check each others' work against answer sheets and help one another with any problems. Final unit tests are taken without teammate help and are scored by student monitors. Each week, teachers total the number of units completed by all team members and give certificates or other team rewards to teams that exceed a criterion score based on the number of final tests passed, with extra points for perfect papers and completed homework.

Because students take responsibility for checking each others' work and managing the flow of materials, the teacher can spend most of the class time presenting lessons to small groups of students drawn from the various teams who are working at the same point in the mathematics sequence. For example, the teacher might call up a decimals group, present a lesson, and then send the students back to their teams to work on problems. Then the teacher might call the fractions group, and so on.

Cooperative Integrated Reading and Composition (CIRC)

The newest of the Student Team Learning methods is a comprehensive program for teaching reading and writing in the upper elementary grades called Cooperative Integrated Reading and Composition (CIRC) (Stevens et al. 1987). In CIRC, teachers use basal or literature-based readers and reading groups, much as in traditional reading programs. However, all students are assigned to teams composed of two pairs from two different reading groups. For example, a team might have two "Bluebirds" and two "Redbirds." While the teacher is working with one reading group, the paired students in the other groups are working on a series of cognitively engaging activities, including reading to one another, making predictions about how narrative stories will come out, summarizing stories to one another, writing responses to stories, and practicing spelling, decoding, and vocabulary. If the reading class is not divided into homogeneous reading groups, all students in the teams work with one another. Students work as a total team to master "main idea" and other comprehension skills. During language arts periods, students engage in writing drafts, revising and editing one another's work, and preparing for "publication" of team books.

In most CIRC activities, students follow a sequence of teacher instruction, team practice, team preassessments, and quizzes. That is, students do not take the quiz until their teammates have determined that they are ready. Certificates are given to teams based on the average performance of all team members on all reading and writing activities.

Other Cooperative Learning Methods

Jigsaw

Jigsaw was originally designed by Elliot Aronson and his colleagues (1978). In Aronson's Jigsaw method, students are assigned to six-member teams to work on academic material that has been broken down into sections. For example, a biography might be divided into early life, first accomplishments, major setbacks, later life, and impact on history. Each team member reads his or her section. Next, members of different teams who have studied the same sections meet in "expert groups" to discuss their sections. Then the students return to their teams and take turns teaching their teammates about their sections. Since the only way students can learn sections other than their own is to listen carefully to their teammates, they are motivated to support and show interest in one another's work. Slavin (1986) developed a modification of jigsaw at Johns Hopkins University and then incorporated it in the Student Team Learning program. In this method, called Jigsaw II, students work in four- or five-member teams as in TGT and STAD. Instead of each student's being assigned a particular section of text, all students read a common narrative, such as a book chapter, a short story, or a biography. However, each student receives a topic (such as "climate" in a unit on France) on which to become an expert. Students with the same topics meet in expert groups to discuss them, after which they return to their teams to teach what they have learned to their teammates. Then students take individual quizzes, which result in team scores based on the improvement score system of STAD. Teams that meet preset standards earn certificates. Jigsaw is primarily used in social studies and other subjects where learning from text is important.

Learning Together

David Johnson and Roger Johnson at the University of Minnesota developed the Learning Together models of cooperative learning (Johnson and Johnson 1987). The methods they have researched involve students working on assignment sheets in four-or five-member heterogeneous groups. The groups hand in a single sheet and receive praise and rewards based on the group product. Their methods emphasize team-building activities before students begin working together and regular discussions within groups about how well they are working together.

Group Investigation

Group Investigation, developed by Shlomo Sharan and Yael Sharan at the University of Tel-Aviv, is a general classroom organization plan in which students work in small groups using cooperative inquiry, group discussion, and cooperative planning and projects (Sharan and Sharan 1976). In this method, students form their own two-to six-member groups. After choosing subtopics from a unit being studied by the entire class, the groups further break their subtopics into individual tasks and carry out the activities necessary to prepare group reports. Each group then makes a presentation or display to communicate its findings to the entire class.

RESEARCH ON COOPERATIVE LEARNING

Cooperative learning methods are among the most extensively evaluated alternatives to traditional instruction in use today. Outcome evaluations include:
- Academic achievement
- Intergroup relations
- Mainstreaming
- Self-esteem
- Others

Academic Achievement

More than 70 high-quality studies have evaluated various cooperative learning methods over periods of at least four weeks in regular elementary and secondary schools; 67 of these have measured effects on student achievement (see Slavin 1990c). All these studies compared the effects of cooperative learning to those of traditionally taught control groups on measures of the same objectives pursued in all classes. Teachers and classes were either randomly assigned to cooperative or control conditions or matched on pretest achievement level and other factors.

Overall, of 67 studies of the achievement effects of cooperative learning, 41 (61 percent) found significantly greater achievement in cooperative than in control classes. Twenty-five (37 percent) found no differences, and in only one study did the control group outperform the experimental group. However, the effects of cooperative learning vary considerably according to the particular methods used. As noted earlier, two elements must be present if cooperative learning is to be effective: *group goals* and *individual accountability* (Slavin 1983a, 1983b, 1990c). That is, groups must be working to achieve some goal or to earn rewards or recognition, and the success of the group must depend on the individual learning of every group member.

In studies of methods such as STAD, TGT, TAI, and CIRC, effects on achievement have been consistently positive; 37 out of 44 such studies (84 percent) found significant positive achievement effects. In contrast, only 4 of 23 studies (17 percent) lacking group goals and individual accountability found positive effects on student achievement. Two of these positive effects were found in studies of Group Investigation in Israel (Sharan et al. 1984; Sharan and Shachar 1988). In Group Investigation, students in each group are responsible for one unique part of the group's overall task, ensuring individual accountability. Then the group's overall performance is evaluated. Even though there are no specific group rewards, the group evaluation probably serves the same purpose.

Why are group goals and individual accountability so important? To understand this, consider the alternatives. In some forms of cooperative learning, students work together to complete a single worksheet or to solve one problem together. In such methods, there is little reason for more able students to take time to explain what is going on to their less able groupmates or to ask their opinions. When the group task is to *do* something, rather than to *learn* something, the participation of less able students may be seen as interference rather than help. It may be easier in this circumstance for students to give each other answers than to explain concepts or skills to one another.

In contrast, when the group's task is to ensure that every group member *learns* something, it is in the interests of every group member to spend time explaining concepts to his or her groupmates. Studies of students' behaviors within cooperative groups have consistently found that the students who gain most from cooperative work are those who give and receive elaborated explanations (Webb 1985). In contrast, Webb found that giving and receiving answers without explanations were *negatively* related to achievement gain. What group goals and individual accountability do is to motivate students to give explanations and to take one another's learning seriously, instead of simply giving answers.

Cooperative learning methods generally work equally well for all types of students. While occasional studies find particular advantages for high or low achievers, boys or girls, and so on, the great majority find equal benefits for all types of students. Sometimes teachers or parents worry that cooperative learning will hold back high achievers. The research provides absolutely no support for this claim; high achievers gain from cooperative learning (relative to high achievers in traditional classes) just as much as do low and average achievers.

Research on the achievement effects of cooperative learning has more often taken place in grades 3–9 than 10–12. Studies at the senior high school level are about as positive as those at earlier grade levels, but there is a need for more research at that level. Cooperative learning methods have been equally successful in urban, rural, and suburban schools and with students of different ethnic groups (although a few studies have found particularly positive effects for Black students; see Slavin and Oickle 1981).

Among the cooperative learning methods, the Student Team Learning programs have been most extensively researched and most often found instructionally effective. Of 14 studies of STAD and closely related methods, 11 found significantly higher achievement for this method than for traditional instruction, and two found no differences. For example, Slavin and Karweit (1984) evaluated STAD over an entire school year in inner-city Philadelphia 9th grade mathematics classes. Student performance on a standardized mathematics test increased significantly more than in either a mastery learning group or a control group using the same materials. Substantial differences favoring STAD have been found in such diverse subjects as social studies (e.g., Allen and VanSickle 1984), language arts (Slavin and Karweit 1981), reading comprehension (Stevens et al. 1988), mathematics (Sherman and Thomas 1986), and science (Okebukola 1985). Nine of 11 studies of TGT found similar results (DeVries and Slavin 1978).

The largest effects of Student Team Learning methods have been found in studies of TAI. Five of six studies found substantially greater learning of mathematics computations in TAI than in control classes, while one study found no differences (see Slavin 1985c). Experimental control differences were still substantial (though smaller) a year after the students were in TAI (Slavin and Karweit 1985). In mathematics concepts and applications, one of three studies (Slavin et al. 1984) found significantly greater gains in TAI than control methods, while two found no significant differences (Slavin and Karweit 1985).

In comparison with traditional control groups, three experimental studies of CIRC have found substantial positive effects on scores from standardized tests of reading comprehension, reading vocabulary, language expression, language mechanics, and spelling (Madden, Stevens, and Slavin 1986a; Stevens et al. 1987; Stevens, Slavin, and Farnish 1990). Significantly greater achievement on writing samples was also found favoring the CIRC students in the two studies which assessed writing.

Other than STL methods, the most consistently successful model for increasing student achievement is Group Investigation (Sharan and Sharan 1976). One study of this method (Sharan et al. 1984) found that it increased the learning of English as a foreign language, while Sharan and Shachar (1988) found positive effects of Group Investigation on the learning of history and geography. A third study of only three weeks' duration (Sharan, Hertz-Lazarowitz, and Ackerman 1980) also found positive effects on social studies achievement, particularly on higher-level concepts. The Learning Together methods (Johnson and Johnson 1987) have been found instructionally effective when they include the assignment of group grades based on the average of group members' individual quiz scores (e.g., Humphreys, Johnson, and Johnson 1982; Yager, Johnson, and Johnson 1985). Studies of the original Jigsaw method have not generally supported this approach (e.g., Moskowitz et al. 1983); but studies of Jigsaw II, which uses group goals and individual accountability, have shown positive effects (Mattingly and Van Sickle 1990; Ziegler 1981).

Intergroup Relations

In the laboratory research on cooperation, one of the earliest and strongest findings was that people who cooperate learn to like one another (Slavin 1977a). Not surprisingly, the cooperative learning classroom studies have found quite consistently that students express greater liking for their classmates in general as a result of participating in a cooperative learning method (see Slavin 1983a, 1990c). This is important in itself and even more important when the students have different ethnic backgrounds. After all, there is substantial evidence that, left alone, ethnic separateness in schools does not naturally diminish over time (Gerard and Miller 1975).

Social scientists have long advocated interethnic cooperation as a means of ensuring positive intergroup relations in desegregated settings. Contact Theory (Allport 1954), which is in the United States the dominant theory of intergroup relations, predicted that positive intergroup relations would arise from school desegregation if and only if students participated in cooperative, equal-status interaction sanctioned by the school. Research on cooperative learning methods has borne out the predictions of Contact Theory. These techniques emphasize cooperative, equal-status interaction between students of different ethnic backgrounds sanctioned by the school (Slavin 1985a).

In most of the research on intergroup relations, students were asked to list their best friends at the beginning of the study and again at the end. The number of friendship choices students made outside their own ethnic groups was the measure of intergroup relations.

Positive effects on intergroup relations have been found for STAD, TGT, TAI, Jigsaw, Learning Together, and Group Investigation models (Slavin 1985b). Two of these studies, one on STAD (Slavin 1979) and one on Jigsaw II (Ziegler 1981), included follow-ups of intergroup friendships several months after the end of the studies. Both found that students who had been in cooperative learning classes still named significantly more friends outside their own ethnic groups than did students who had been in control classes. Two studies of Group Investigation (Sharan et al. 1984; Sharan and Shachar 1988) found that students' improved attitudes and behaviors toward classmates of different ethnic backgrounds extended to classmates who had never been in the same groups, and a study of TAI (Oishi 1983) found positive effects of this method on cross-ethnic interactions outside as well as in class. The U.S. studies of cooperative learning and intergroup relations involved Black, white, and (in a few cases) Mexican-American students. A study of Jigsaw II by Ziegler (1981) took place in Toronto, where the major ethnic groups were Anglo-Canadians and children of recent European immigrants. The Sharan (Sharan et al., 1984, Sharan and Shachar 1988) studies of Group Investigation took place in Israel and involved friendships between Jews of both European and Middle Eastern backgrounds.

Mainstreaming

Although ethnicity is a major barrier to friendship, it is not so large as the one between physically or mentally handicapped children and their normal-progress peers. Mainstreaming, an unprecedented opportunity for handicapped children to take their place in the school and society, has created enormous practical problems for classroom teachers, and it often leads to social rejection of the handicapped children. Because cooperative learning methods have been successful in improving relationships across the ethnicity barrier—which somewhat resembles the barrier between mainstreamed and normal-progress students—these methods have also been applied to increase the acceptance of the mainstreamed student.

The research on cooperative learning and mainstreaming has focused on the academically handicapped child. In one study, STAD were used to attempt to integrate students performing two years or more below the level of their peers into the social structure of the classroom. The use of STAD significantly reduced the degree to which the normal-progress students rejected their mainstreamed classmates and increased the academic achievement and self-esteem of all students, mainstreamed as well as normal-progress (Madden and Slavin 1983a). Similar effects have been found for TAI (Slavin, Madden, and Leavey 1984), and other research using cooperative teams has also shown significant improvements in relationships between mainstreamed academically handicapped students and their normal-progress peers (Ballard et al. 1977; Cooper et al. 1980).

In addition, one study in a self-contained school for emotionally disturbed adolescents found that the use of TGT increased positive interactions and friendships among students (Slavin 1977c). Five months after the study ended, these positive interactions were still found more often in the former TGT classes than in the control classes. In a study in a similar setting, Janke (1978) found that the emotionally disturbed students were more on-task, were better behaved, and had better attendance in TGT classes than in control classes.

Self-Esteem

One the most important aspects of a child's personality is his or her self-esteem. Several researchers working on cooperative learning techniques have found that these methods do increase students' self-esteem. These improvements in self-esteem have been found for TGT and STAD (Slavin 1990c) for Jigsaw (Blaney et al. 1977), and for the three methods combined (Slavin and Karweit 1981). Improvements in student self-concepts have also been found for TAI (Slavin, Leavey, and Madden 1984).

Other Outcomes

In addition to effects on achievement, positive intergroup relations, greater acceptance of mainstreamed students, and self-esteem, effects of cooperative learning have been found on a variety of other important educational outcomes. These include liking school, development of peer norms in favor of doing well academically, feelings of individual control over the student's own fate in school, and cooperativeness and altruism (see Slavin 1983a, 1990c). TGT (DeVries and Slavin 1978) and STAD (Slavin 1978; Janke 1978) have been found to have positive effects on students' time-on-task. One study found that lower socioeconomic status students at risk of becoming delinquent who worked in cooperative groups in sixth grade had better attendance, fewer contacts with the police, and higher behavioral ratings by teachers in grades 7–11 than did control students (Hartley 1986). Another study implemented forms of cooperative learning beginning in kindergarten and continuing through the fourth grade (Solomon et al. 1990). This study found that the students who had been taught cooperatively were significantly higher than control students on measures of supportive, friendly, and prosocial behavior; were better at resolving conflicts; and expressed more support for democratic values.

USEFUL STRATEGIES

Returning to the question at the beginning of this article, we now see the usefulness of cooperative learning strategies for improving such diverse outcomes as student achievement at a variety of grade levels and in many subjects, intergroup relations, relationships between mainstreamed and normal-progress students, and student self-esteem. Further, their widespread and growing use demonstrates that cooperative learning methods are practical and attractive to teachers. The history of the development, evaluation, and dissemination of cooperative learning is an outstanding example of the use of educational research to create programs that have improved the educational experience of thousands of students and will continue to affect thousands more.

Authors note. This article was written under funding from the Office of Educational Research and Improvement, U.S. Department of Education (Grant No. OERI-R-117-R90002). However, any opinions expressed are mine and do not represent OERI positions or policy.

7. RESEARCH ON COOPERATIVE LEARNING: CONSENSUS AND CONTROVERSY

by Robert E. Slavin

Cooperative learning is one of the most thoroughly researched of all instructional methods. In a recent review (Slavin 1989a), I identified 60 studies that contrasted the achievement outcomes of cooperative learning and traditional methods in elementary and secondary schools. To be included in my review, studies had to have lasted at least four weeks, and experimental and control classes had to take the same achievement tests under the same conditions. Using different inclusion criteria, Johnson and colleagues (1981) identified 122 achievement studies. Most of these studies also measured many outcomes in addition to achievement.

With so many studies, one would imagine that a consensus would emerge about the nature and size of the effects of cooperative learning; and, in fact, the areas of agreement among cooperative learning researchers far outweigh the areas of disagreement. Yet there remain several key points of controversy among researchers and reviewers that concern the conditions under which cooperative learning is instructionally effective. This article briefly summarizes the main areas of consensus and controversy in research on cooperative learning.

COOPERATIVE LEARNING AND STUDENT ACHIEVEMENT

Consensus. There is wide agreement among reviewers of the cooperative learning literature that cooperative methods can and usually do have a positive effect on student achievement. Further, there is almost as strong a consensus that the achievement effects are not seen for all forms of cooperative learning but depend on two essential features, at least at the elementary and secondary levels. One of these features is *group goals*, or positive interdependence: the cooperative groups must work together to earn recognition, grades, rewards, and other indicators of group success. Simply asking students to work together is not enough. The second essential feature is *individual accountability*: the group's success must depend on the individual learning of all group members. For example, group success might depend on the sum of members' quiz scores or on evaluation of a report in which each group member contributed his or her own

This chapter is an article that appeared in the December 1989/January 1990 *Educational Leadership* 47 (4): 52–54. Reprinted with permission of the Association for Supervision and Curriculum Development. Copyright 1989 by the Association for Supervision and Curriculum Development. All rights reserved.

chapter. In contrast, studies of methods in which students work together to prepare a single worksheet or project without differentiated tasks hardly ever find achievement benefits (Slavin 1989a).

The degree of consensus on the achievement effects of cooperative learning methods that use group goals and individual accountability is considerable. I am aware of four full-scale reviews by different authors on this topic. My own reviews (Slavin 1983b, 1989a, 1990c) have focused on elementary and secondary schools. Reviews by the Johnsons (Johnson et al. 1981) have included all levels, including college. Newmann and Thompson (1987) have focused on secondary schools (middle, junior, and high schools), and Davidson (1985) has reviewed research on cooperative learning in mathematics.

The findings of the four reviews were similar. My own concluded, "Cooperative learning can be an effective means of increasing student achievement, but only if group goals and individual accountability are incorporated in the cooperative methods" (Slavin 1989a, p. 151). Newmann and Thompson (1987, pp. 11-12) came to similar conclusions:

> A review of the research on cooperative learning and achievement in grades 7–12 produced 27 reports of high-quality studies, including 37 comparisons of cooperative versus control methods. Twenty-five (68 percent) of these favored a cooperative learning method at the .05 level of significance. . . . The pattern of results supports the importance not only of a cooperative task structure, but also of group rewards of individual accountability, and probably of group competition as well.

Davidson (1985, p. 224) wrote: "If the term *achievement* refers to computational skills, simple concepts, and simple application problems, the studies at the elementary and secondary levels support Slavin's (1983b) conclusions. . . . 'Cooperative learning methods that use group rewards and individual accountability consistently increase student achievement more than control methods in . . . elementary and secondary classrooms.'" All four reviews mentioned group goals and individual accountability as essential elements of cooperative learning.

Controversy. While no reviewer has yet expressed doubt that there is a broad set of conditions under which cooperative learning will increase student achievement, there is controversy about the specific conditions under which positive effects will be found.

One focus of controversy has been a debate between David and Roger Johnson and me that has more to do with different views on what constitutes adequate research than on questions of the essential elements of cooperative learning. The main elements of this debate have been covered in earlier issues of *Educational Leadership* (see Slavin 1988a, Johnson and Johnson 1989; Slavin 1989b).

In addition to the controversy between the Johnsons and me, several other issues have been raised by various writers and reviewers. One issue is whether cooperative learning is effective at all grade levels. Newmann and Thompson (1987) question whether cooperative learning is effective in senior high school (grades 10–12). There is ample evidence that these methods are instructionally effective in grades 2–9, but relatively few studies examine grades 10–12. More research is needed in this area.

Another issue is the effects of cooperative learning at the college level. Again, there are relatively few studies at this level, and the results are not as consistent as those from elementary and junior high/middle schools. However, there are several examples of positive achievement effects of cooperative learning in senior high school and college settings (see, for example, Sherman and Thomas 1986; Fraser et al. 1977).

Another question being debated is the appropriateness of cooperative learning for higher-order conceptual learning. Most cooperative learning studies have focused on basic skills (mathematics, language arts, reading), but several have successfully taught such higher-order skills as creative writing (Stevens et al. 1987) and identification of main idea and inference in reading (Stevens et al. 1988). Studies of Sharan's Group Investigation method (see for example, Sharan, Hertz-Lazarowitz, and Ackerman 1980) and of the Johnsons' constructive controversy methods (see, for example, Smith, Johnson, and Johnson 1981) have reported particularly strong effects on higher-order understanding in social studies.

Davidson (1985) has questioned whether group goals and individual accountability are necessary at the college level, and there is some evidence that they may not be. Studies of pair learning of text comprehension strategies by Dansereau (1988), as well as some of the mathematics studies cited by Davidson (1985), provide examples of successful use of cooperative learning at the college level without group goals or individual accountability.

OUTCOMES OTHER THAN ACHIEVEMENT

In areas other than achievement, there is even broader consensus about the effects of cooperative learning. One of the most consistent of these is the effect on intergroup relations (see Slavin 1985a; Johnson, Johnson, and Marvyama 1983). When students of different racial or ethnic backgrounds work together toward a common goal, they gain in liking and respect for one another. Cooperative learning also improves the social acceptance of mainstreamed academically handicapped students by their classmates (Madden and Slavin 1983b; Johnson, Johnson, and Marvyama 1983), as well as increasing friendships among students in general (Slavin 1990).

Other outcomes seen in many studies of cooperative learning include gains in self-esteem, liking of school and of the subject being studied, time-on-task, and attendance (Slavin 1990). Studies by Sharan and colleagues (1984) have shown that extended experiences with cooperative learning can increase the ability to work effectively with others.

101

BASIC AGREEMENT

In every area of research there are debates about what the research means. Cooperative learning, a topic studied by many researchers from different research traditions, is certainly no exception. However, after nearly two decades of research and scores of studies, a considerable degree of consensus has emerged. There is agreement that—at least in elementary and middle/junior high schools and with basic skills objectives—cooperative methods that incorporate group goals and individual accountability accelerate student learning considerably. Further, there is agreement that these methods have positive effects on a wide array of affective outcomes, such as intergroup relations, acceptance of mainstreamed students, and self-esteem.

Research must continue to test the limits of cooperative learning, to broaden our understanding of why and how cooperative learning produces its various effects (see Bossert 1988–89). Yet what we know already is more than enough to justify expanded use of cooperative learning as a routine and central feature of instruction.

Author's note. Preparation of this article was supported by a grant from the Office of Educational Research and Improvement, U.S. Department of Education (No. OERIG-86-0006). However, any opinions expressed are mine and do not represent OERI positions or policy.

8. ARE COOPERATIVE LEARNING AND "UNTRACKING" HARMFUL TO THE GIFTED?

by Robert E. Slavin

In the past few years there has been remarkably rapid development in American education on two distinct but related fronts. One is the adoption of various forms of cooperative learning, and the other is the search for alternatives to traditional tracking and ability-grouping practices. Cooperative learning and "untracking" have completely different rationales, research bases, and political and practical implications. Cooperative learning can work within a completely tracked school, and untracking by no means requires cooperative learning. Yet the two movements have become intertwined in the minds of educators because cooperative learning is often offered as one means of teaching the very heterogeneous classes created by untracking and because of a widespread assumption that if homogeneous large groups are bad, then heterogeneous small groups must be good. Perhaps I have contributed to the confusion by having written in support of both practices (see, for example, Slavin 1988b and Chapter 6 in this publication).

In education, there is no fundamental change that does not generate enemies. In the case of both untracking and cooperative learning, opposition is now developing among members of the same group: researchers, educators, and parents concerned about the education of gifted children. For example, recently in *ASCD Update*, cooperative learning was cited by several researchers and educators involved in gifted education as having a detrimental effect on the gifted, both in that the cooperative learning movement has often led to abandonment of separate gifted programs and in the gifted students "report feeling used, resentful, and frustrated by group work with students of lower ability" (Willis 1990, p. 8). And in *Educational Leadership*, Susan Allan (1991) writes that "gifted and high-ability children show positive academic effects from some forms of homogeneous grouping" (p. 64).

The questions of untracking and cooperative learning for the gifted are important for others besides the 5 percent (or so) of students who are identified as academically gifted because arguments about the gifted are often used to defeat attempts to reduce or eliminate tracking with the remaining 95 percent of students.

What is the evidence on ability grouping and cooperative learning for gifted or other high-ability students? In this article I discuss the research and the logic around these issues of programming for very able students.

IS UNTRACKING BAD FOR HIGH ACHIEVERS?

Leaving aside the question of cooperative learning or other instructional strategies, it is important to understand what has been found in the research on ability grouping in general. Susan Allen correctly observes that the popular press has distorted the research, making ability grouping appear disastrous for the achievement of all students. She is also correct in noting that different ability grouping practices have different achievement effects (see Slavin 1988b). However, I strongly disagree with her conclusion that ability grouping is beneficial to high achievers and her implication that it is therefore a desirable practice.

First, let me make a critical distinction between "high achievers" and the "gifted." In most studies, high achievers are the top 33 percent of students; gifted are more often the top 3 to 5 percent. These are very different groups, and I will address them separately.

Is ability grouping beneficial for high-ability students? My reviews of research on between-class ability grouping (tracking) found it was not. In elementary studies I found a median effect size for high achievers of +.04, which is trivially different from zero (Slavin 1987a).[1] In secondary schools, the effect was +.01 (Slavin 1990b). Kulik and Kulik (1987) obtained medians of +.10 in elementary, +.09 in secondary schools—higher than mine, but still very small. Most reviewers consider an effect size less than +.20 to be educationally insignificant. In almost every study I reviewed, the achievement differences between ability-grouped and heterogeneous placement were not statistically significant for high achievers. The possibility that the failure to find educationally meaningful effects could be due to ceiling effects on standardized tests is remote; standardized tests are certainly designed to measure adequately the achievement of the top 33 percent of students.

Now let's consider the gifted, the top 3 to 5 percent of students. Gifted programs fall into two categories: *enrichment* and *acceleration*. In acceleration programs, students either skip a grade or take courses not usually offered at their grade level (for example, Algebra I in seventh grade.) When acceleration involves only one subject, that subject is almost always mathematics. All other gifted programs, which do not involve skipping grades or courses, are called enrichment.

Research on acceleration does favor the practice (see Kulik and Kulik 1984), although this research is difficult to interpret. If one student takes Algebra I and a similar student takes Math 7, the Algebra I student will obviously do better on an algebra test. Still, studies of this type find that the accelerated students do almost as well as non-accelerated students on, say, tests of Math 7, so the extra algebra learning is probably a real benefit.

---

[1]In this case, an "effect size" is the difference between ability grouped and ungrouped students on achievement tests divided by the test's standard deviation. Effect sizes between -.20 and +.20 are generally considered to indicate no meaningful differences.

Research on enrichment programs, which are far more common in practice, is, to put it mildly, a mess. Most such studies compare students assigned to a gifted program to students who were not so assigned, often to students who were *rejected* from the same programs! Such studies usually control statistically for IQ or prior achievement, but these controls are inadequate. Imagine two students with IQs of 130, one assigned to a gifted program, the other rejected. Can they be considered equivalent? Of course not—the rejected student was probably lower in motivation, actual achievement, or other factors highly relevant to the student's likely progress (see Slavin 1984). A study by Howell (1962), included in the Kulik and Kulik (1982, 1987) meta-analyses, compared students in gifted classes to those rejected for the same program, controlling for nothing. The only study I know of that randomly assigned gifted students to gifted (enrichment) or heterogeneous classes (Mikkelson 1962) found small differences favoring *heterogeneous* placement. Reviewers of the literature on effects of gifted programs (for example, Fox 1979) have generally concluded that while acceleration programs do enhance achievement, enrichment programs do not. Even if enrichment programs were ultimately found to be effective for gifted students, this would still leave open the possibility that they would be just as effective for *all* students (Slavin 1990a).

Leaving aside for a moment the special case of acceleration, nearly all researchers would agree that the achievement effects of between-class ability grouping (tracking) for all students are small to nil. What does this say to the practitioner? Since arguments for ability grouping depend entirely on the belief that grouping increases achievement, the absence of such evidence undermines any rationale for the practice. The harm done by ability groups, I believe, lies not primarily in effects on achievement but in other impacts on low and average achievers. For example, low-track students are more likely to be delinquent or to drop out of school than similar low achievers not in the low track (Wiatrowski et al. 1982). Perhaps most important, tracking works against our national ideology that all are created equal and our desire to be one nation. The fact that African-American, Hispanic, and low socioeconomic students in general wind up so often in the low tracks is repugnant on its face. Why would we want to organize our schools this way if we have no evidence that it helps students learn?

I do believe that schools must recognize individual differences and allow all students to reach their full potential, and they can do this by using flexible within-class grouping strategies and other instructional techniques without turning to across-the-board between-class grouping (see Slavin et al. 1989). In some cases (mostly mathematics), acceleration may be justified for extremely able students. But the great majority of students can and should learn together.

IS COOPERATIVE LEARNING BAD FOR HIGH ACHIEVERS?

In research on cooperative learning, we have routinely analyzed achievement outcomes according to students' pretest scores. Those in the top third, middle third, and low third have all gained consistently, relative to similar students in control classes, as long as the cooperative learning program in use provides group goals and individual accountability (see Chapter 6 in this publication). High achievers gain from cooperative learning in part because their peers encourage them to learn (it benefits the group) and because, as any teacher knows, we learn best by describing our current state of knowledge to others (see Webb 1985).

In preparation for writing this article, I asked my colleague, Robert Stevens, to run some additional analyses on a study he is doing in two suburban elementary schools. The two schools have been using cooperative learning in all academic subjects for many years, in which all forms of between-class ability grouping are avoided and in which special education teachers team with regular classroom teachers to teach classes containing both academically handicapped and non-handicapped students. Stevens' analyses focused on three definitions of high ability: top 33 percent, top 10 percent, and top 5 percent. The results for grades two to five on standardized tests are summarized in Figure 1.

Figure 1: Difference in Effect Sizes Between High Achievers in Two Cooperative and Two Control Schools

Measure	Top 33%	Top 10%	Top 5%
Reading Vocabulary	+.42	+.65	+.32
Reading Comprehension	+.53	+.68	+.96
Language Mechanics	+.28	+.11	−.14
Language Expression	+.28	+.48	+.17
Math Computation	+.63	+.59	+.62
Math Concepts and Applications	+.28	+.32	+.19

Note: These data are from Point Pleasant and Overlook Elementary Schools and two matched comparison schools in Anne Arundel County, Maryland, a Baltimore suburb.

Figure 1 shows that even the very highest achieving students benefited from cooperative learning in comparison to similar students in the two control schools. The only exception was on Language Mechanics, probably because the writing process approach we use does not emphasize mechanics out of the context of writing. It is important to note that the Stevens study does not involve run-of-the-mill cooperative learning in reading, writing/language arts, or mathematics, but uses Cooperative Integrated Reading and Composition or CIRC (Stevens et al. 1987) and Team-Assisted Individualization (TAI) Mathematics (Slavin 1985b; also see Chapter 9 in this publication). These programs incorporate flexible grouping within the class and therefore differentiate instruction for students of different achievement levels. Still, no separate grouping or special program was needed to accelerate substantially the achievement of even the highest achievers (and of other students as well).

Many of the concerns expressed about high achievers in cooperative learning are based either on misconceptions or on experience with inappropriate forms of cooperative learning. First, many educators and parents worry that high achievers will be used as "junior teachers" instead of being able to move ahead on their own material. This is a confusion of cooperative learning with peer tutoring; in all cooperative methods, students are learning material that is new to all of them. A related concern is that high achievers will be held back waiting for their groupmates. This is perhaps a concern about untracking, but not about cooperative learning. In cooperative learning students are typically exposed to the same content they would have seen anyway; and in forms of cooperative learning such as CIRC and TAI, they may progress far more rapidly than they otherwise would have. Sometimes parents are concerned when their youngsters' grades are made dependent on those of their groupmates. This does happen in some forms of cooperative learning, but I am personally very opposed to the practice. Certificates or other recognition work just as well, and grades can and should be given based on individual performance.

NO EVIDENCE IN FAVOR OF TRACKING

My personal philosophy of education is that all students should be helped to achieve their full potential. I am in favor of acceleration programs (especially in mathematics) for the gifted, and I believe in differentiating instruction *within* heterogeneous classes to meet the needs of students above (and below) the class average in performance. But I see no evidence or logic to support separate enrichment programs for gifted students. Enrichment is appropriate for *all* students. I see little evidence at all for separate tracks for high achievers. The burden of proof for the antidemocratic, antiegalitarian practice of ability grouping must be on those who would group, and no one who reads this literature could responsibly conclude that this requirement has been met.

The likely impact of untracking per se on the achievement of high achievers is no impact at all: these students will do well wherever they are. However, with the use of effective cooperative learning programs, especially those that differentiate instruction within the class, high achievers are likely to benefit in achievement, even the very top-achieving 5 percent. Educators of the gifted should be in the forefront of the cooperative learning movement, insisting on the use of forms of cooperative learning known to benefit gifted and other able students. If these methods also happen to be good for average and below average students, so much the better!

Author's note. This article was written under a grant from the Office of Educational Research and Improvement, U.S. Department of Education (No. OERI-R-117-R90002). However, any opinions expressed are mine and do not represent OERI positions or policies.

9. COOPERATIVE LEARNING MODELS FOR THE 3 R's

by Robert E. Slavin, Nancy A. Madden, and Robert J. Stevens

In 1980 at Johns Hopkins University we began to develop and evaluate cooperative learning programs designed specifically for particular subjects and grade levels. We set out with several critical objectives. First, we wanted to use what we had learned about cooperative learning to try to solve fundamental problems of instruction, such as accommodating individual differences in reading and math. In particular, we wanted to design programs that could be used in heterogeneous classes, to reduce the need for special education or tracking. Second, we wanted to design cooperative learning programs that could be used all year, not just from time to time as part of a teacher's bag of tricks. Third, we wanted to incorporate knowledge about curriculum- and domain-specific learning into our cooperative approaches, such as the teaching of story grammar and summarizing in reading, or the writing process in writing.

The programs we developed, Team Assisted Individualization (TAI) in mathematics and Cooperative Integrated Reading and Composition (CIRC), are among the best researched and most effective of all cooperative learning methods. This article describes TAI and CIRC and the research on them.

TEAM ASSISTED INDIVIDUALIZATION

The first comprehensive cooperative learning model we developed and researched was Team Assisted Individualization—Mathematics,[1] a program that combines cooperative learning with individualized instruction to meet the needs of diverse classrooms (Slavin 1985b).

We developed TAI for several reasons. First, we hoped TAI would provide a means of combining the motivational power and peer assistance of cooperative learning with an individualized instructional program—one that would provide all students with materials appropriate to their levels of skill and allow them to proceed through these materials at their own rates. Second, TAI was developed to apply cooperative learning techniques to solve many of the problems of individualized instruction.

In the 1960s, individualized instruction and related methods had been expected to revolutionize instruction, especially in mathematics. However,

This chapter is an article that appeared in the December 1989/January 1990 *Educational Leadership* 47 (4): 22-28. Reprinted with permission of the Association for Supervision and Curriculum Development. Copyright 1989 by the Association for Supervision and Curriculum Development. All rights reserved.

reviews of the research on these instruction methods in mathematics have consistently concluded that these methods are no more effective than traditional instruction (see, for example, Miller 1976; Horak 1981). Several problems inherent in programmed instruction have been cited as contributing to these disappointing findings: too much time spent on management rather than teaching, too little incentive for students to progress rapidly through the programmed materials, and excessive reliance on written instruction rather than instruction from a teacher.

We felt that by combining programmed instruction with cooperative learning and turning most of the management functions (for example, scoring answers, locating and filing materials, keeping records, assigning new work) over to the students themselves, these problems could be solved. If students could handle most of the checking and management, the teacher would be free to teach individuals and small homogeneous teaching groups. Students working in learning teams toward a cooperative goal could help one another study, provide instant feedback to one another, and encourage one another to proceed rapidly and accurately through the materials.

Finally, TAI was developed as a means of producing the well-documented social effects characteristic of cooperative learning (Slavin 1990c) while meeting diverse needs. Our principal concern here was mainstreaming. We felt that mainstreaming of academically handicapped students in mathematics was limited by the belief of regular class teachers that they were unprepared to accommodate the instructional needs of these students (see Gickling and Theobald 1975). Further, studies of attitudes toward academically handicapped students had consistently found that these students are not well accepted by their nonhandicapped classmates (see Gottlieb and Leyser 1981).

Since cooperative learning methods have had positive effects on social relations of all kinds, specifically on relationships between handicapped and nonhandicapped students (Madden and Slavin 1983b), we felt that the best possible mathematics program for the mainstreamed classroom would be one that combined cooperative learning with individualized instruction (see Madden and Slavin 1983b). Recently, as many districts have moved away from tracking toward heterogeneous classes, the need for effective programs that can accommodate mathematics instruction to diverse needs has increased.

Principal Features of TAI

TAI is designed primarily for grades 3 to 6, but it has been used at higher grade levels (up to the community college level) for groups of students not ready for a full algebra course. It is almost always used without aides, volunteers, or other assistance. The principal elements of TAI are as follows (adapted from Slavin, Leavy, and Madden 1986):

Teams. Students are assigned to four- to five-member teams. Each team has a mix of high, average, and low achievers, boys and girls, and students of any ethnic groups in the class. Every eight weeks, students are reassigned to new teams.

Placement test. At the beginning of the program, students are pretested on mathematics operations. They are placed at the appropriate point in the individualized program based on their performance on the placement test.

Curriculum materials. Following instruction from the teacher (see "Teaching groups," below), students work in their teams on self-instructional curriculum materials covering addition, subtraction, multiplication, division, numeration, decimals, fractions, word problems, statistics, and algebra. The units are in the form of books. Each unit has the following parts:

- A guide page that reviews the teacher's lesson, explaining the skill to be mastered and giving a step-by-step method for solving the problems.
- Several skill practice pages, each consisting of 16 problems. Each skill practice page introduces a subskill that leads to a final mastery of the entire skill.
- Formative tests A and B (two parallel 10-item sets).
- A unit test of 15 items.
- Answer sheets for the skill practice pages and formative tests (located at the back of student books) and answers for unit tests (located in a separate "monitor book").

Word problems are emphasized throughout the materials.

Teaching groups. Every day, the teacher teaches lessons to small groups of students (drawn from the heterogeneous teams) who are at the same point in the curriculum. Teachers use specific concept lessons provided as part of the program. The purpose of these sessions is to introduce major concepts to the students. Teachers make extensive use of manipulatives, diagrams, and demonstrations. The lessons are designed to help students understand the connection between the mathematics they are doing and familiar real-life problems.

While the teacher works with a teaching group, the other students continue to work in their teams on their self-instructional units. This direct instruction to teaching groups is possible because students take responsibility for almost all checking, handling of materials, and routing.

Team study method. Following the placement test, the students are given a starting place in the sequence of mathematics units. They work on their units in their teams, using the following steps:

1. Students locate their units within their books and read the guide page, asking teammates or the teacher for help if necessary. Then the students begin with the first skill practice page in their unit.
2. Each student works the first four problems on his or her own skill practice page and then has a teammate check the answers against an answer sheet printed upside-down at the back of each student book. If all four are correct, the student may go on to the next skill practice page. If any are incorrect, the student must try the

next four problems, and so on, until he or she gets one block of four problems correct. If they run into difficulties at this stage, students are encouraged to ask for help within their teams before asking the teacher for help.

3. When a student gets four in a row correct on the last skill practice page, he or she takes Formative Test A, a 10-item quiz that resembles the last skill practice page. Students work alone on the test until they are finished. A teammate scores the formative test. If the student gets eight or more of the 10 problems correct, the teammate signs the student's paper to indicate that the student is certified by the team to take the unit test. If the student does not get eight correct (this is rare), the teacher is called in to respond to any problems the student is having. The teacher would diagnose the student's problem and briefly reteach the skill, possibly asking the student to work again on certain skill practice items. The student then takes Formative Test B, a second 10-item test comparable in content and difficulty to Formative Test A.

4. When a student passes Formative Test A or B, he or she takes the test paper to a student monitor from a different team to get the appropriate unit test. The student then completes the unit test, and the monitor scores it. Two different students serve as monitors each day. If the student gets at least 12 items correct (out of 15), the monitor posts the score on the student's Team Summary sheet. Otherwise, the test is examined by the teacher, who meets with the student to diagnose and remediate the student's problems. Again, because students have already shown mastery on the skill practice pages and formative tests, they rarely fail a unit test.

Team scores and team recognition. At the end of each week, the teacher computes a team score. This score is based on the average number of units covered by each team member and the accuracy of the unit tests. Criteria are established for team performance. A high criterion is set for a team to be a "superteam," a moderate criterion is set for a team to be a "greatteam," and a minimum criterion is set for a team to be a "goodteam." The teams meeting the "superteam" and "greatteam" criteria receive attractive certificates.

Facts tests. Twice each week, the students are given three-minute facts tests (usually multiplication or division facts). The students are given fact sheets to study at home to prepare for these tests.

Whole-class units. Every three weeks, the teacher stops the individualized program and spends a week teaching lessons to the entire class covering such skills as geometry, measurement, sets, and problem-solving strategies.

Research on TAI

Seven field experiments have evaluated the effects of TAI on student achievement, attitudes, and behavior (see Slavin 1985a). Academic achievement outcomes were assessed in six of the seven studies. In five of these, TAI students significantly[2] exceeded control students on standardized (CTBS or CAT) Math Computations scales. Similar effects were found for Concepts and Applications in only one of the four studies in which this variable was assessed; but in all four studies, means for Concepts and Applications favored the TAI group. In the five studies in which the treatment effects for Computations were statistically significant, they were also quite large; on average, TAI classes gained twice as many grade equivalents as did control students. Effects of TAI were equally positive for high, average, and low achievers, and for academically handicapped as well as nonhandicapped students. Positive effects of TAI have also been found on such outcomes as self-concept in math, liking for math class, classroom behavior, race relations, and acceptance of mainstreamed academically handicapped students (Slavin 1985a).

COOPERATIVE INTEGRATED READING AND COMPOSITION

Following the success of the TAI mathematics program, we turned to reading and writing/language arts, the two subjects that, with mathematics, constitute the core of the elementary school program. Because these subjects are very different from mathematics, our approach to applying cooperative learning to them was very different. For one thing, reading, writing, and language arts include subskills that each demand different approaches. For example, optimal procedures for teaching reading comprehension or vocabulary would certainly be different from those for teaching decoding, spelling, writing, or language mechanics.

The program we ultimately developed and researched is called Cooperative Integrated Reading and Composition, or CIRC (Madden et al. 1986,1988). Our development plan focused on using cooperative learning as a vehicle to introduce practices identified in recent research on reading and writing into routine classroom practice, and to embed cooperative learning within the fabric of the elementary reading and writing program (see Stevens et al. 1987).

Principal Features of CIRC

The CIRC program includes three principal elements: basal-related activities, direct instruction in reading comprehension, and integrated language arts/writing. In all of these activities, students work in heterogeneous learning teams.

Reading groups. Students are assigned to two or three reading groups (8–15 students per group) according to their reading level, as determined by their teachers.

Teams. Students are assigned to pairs (or triads) within their reading groups. The pairs are then assigned to teams composed of partnerships from two different reading groups. For example, a team might be composed of two students from the top reading group and two from the low group. Mainstreamed academically handicapped and remedial reading (for example, Chapter I) students are distributed among the teams.

Many of the activities within the teams are done in pairs, while others involve the whole team; even during pair activities, however, the other pair is available for assistance and encouragement. Most of the time, the teams work independently of the teacher, while the teacher either teaches reading groups drawn from the various teams or works with individuals. Students scores on all quizzes, compositions, and book reports contribute to a team score. Teams that meet an average criterion of 90 percent on all activities in a given week are designated "superteams" and receive attractive certificates; those that meet an average criterion of 80 to 89 percent are designated "greatteams" and receive less elaborate certificates.

Basal-related activities. Students use their regular basal readers (or whatever texts or reading materials are used in the school). Stories are introduced and discussed in teacher-led reading groups that meet for approximately 20 minutes each day. During these sessions, teachers set a purpose for reading, introduce new vocabulary, review old vocabulary, discuss the story after students have read it, and so on. Presentation methods for each segment of the lesson are structured. For example, teachers are taught to use a vocabulary presentation procedure that requires a demonstration of understanding of word meaning by each individual, a review of methods of word attack, repetitive oral reading of vocabulary to achieve automaticity, and use of the meanings of the vocabulary words to help introduce the content of the story. Story discussions are structured to emphasize such skills as making and supporting predictions about the story and understanding major structural components of the story (for example, problem and solution in a narrative).

After the stories are introduced, the students are given a series of activities to do in their teams when they are not working with the teacher in a reading group. The sequence of activities is as follows:

1. *Partner reading.* First, students read the story silently, then take turns reading the story aloud with their partners, alternating readers after each paragraph. As his or her partner reads, the listener follows along and corrects any errors the reader makes.

2. *Story structure and story-related writing.* Students are given questions related to each narrative that emphasize story grammar. Halfway through the story, they are instructed to stop reading and to identify the characters, the setting, and the problem in the story, and to predict how the problem will be resolved. At the end

of the story, students respond to the story as a whole and write a few paragraphs on a topic related to the story (for example, they might be asked to write a different ending to the story).

3. *Words out loud.* Students are given a list of new or difficult words used in the story, which they must be able to read correctly in any order without hesitating or stumbling. These words are presented by the teacher in the reading group, and then students practice their lists with their partners or other teammates until they can read them smoothly.

4. *Word meaning.* Students are given a list of story words that are new in their speaking vocabularies. They look them up in a dictionary, paraphrase the definitions, and write a sentence for each that shows the meaning of the word (i.e., "An octopus grabbed the swimmer with its eight long legs," not "I have an octopus").

5. *Story retell.* After reading the story and discussing it in their reading groups, students summarize the main points of the story to their partners. The partners have a list of essential story elements, which they use to check the completeness of the story summaries.

6. *Spelling.* Students pretest one another on a list of spelling words each week, and then work over the course of the week to help one another master the list. Students use a "disappearing list" strategy in which they make new lists of missed words after each assessment until the list disappears, and they can go back to the full list, repeating the process as many times as necessary.

Partner checking. After students complete the activities listed above, their partners initial a student assignment form indicating that they have completed or achieved criterion on that task. Students are given daily expectations as to the number of activities to be completed, but they can go at their own rate and complete the activities earlier if they wish, creating additional time for independent reading (see below).

Tests. At the end of three class periods, students are given a comprehension test on the story, are asked to write meaningful sentences for each vocabulary word, and are asked to read the word list aloud to the teacher. Students are not permitted to help one another on these tests. The test scores and evaluations of the story-related writing are major components of students' weekly team scores.

Direct instruction in reading comprehension. One day each week, students receive direct instruction from the teacher in reading comprehension skills such as identifying main ideas, drawing conclusions, and comparing and contrasting ideas. A special curriculum was designed for this purpose. After each lesson, students work on reading comprehension worksheets or games as a whole team, first gaining consensus on one set of worksheet items, then practicing independently, assessing one another's work, and discussing any remaining problems on a second set of items.

Independent reading. Students are asked to read a trade book of their choice every evening for at least 20 minutes. Parents initial forms indicating that students have read for the required time, and students contribute points to their teams if they submit a completed form each week. Students complete at least one book report every two weeks, for which they also receive team points. Independent reading and book reports replace all other homework in reading and language arts. If students complete their basal-related activities or other activities early, they may also read their independent reading books in class.

Integrated language arts and writing. During language arts periods, teachers use a specific language arts/writing curriculum developed for the project. Students work on language arts in the same teams as in reading. During three one-hour sessions each week, students participate in a writers' workshop (Graves 1983), writing at their own pace on topics of their choice. Teachers present 10-minute minilessons at the beginning of each period on the writing process, style, or mechanics; for example, brainstorming for topics, conducting a peer revision conference, eliminating run-on sentences, or using quotations. Students spend the main part of the period planning, drafting, revising, editing, or publishing their writing.

Informal and formal peer and teacher conferences are held during this time. Ten minutes at the end of the hour are reserved for sharing and "celebration" of student writing. Teacher-directed lessons on specific aspects of writing, such as organizing a narrative or a descriptive paragraph, using specific sensory words in a description, and ensuring noun-verb agreement, are conducted during two periods each week, and students practice and master these skills in their teams.

Involvement of special education resource teachers and reading teachers. One key concern in the design of the CIRC program was to fully integrate the activities of special education resource teachers and remedial reading teachers (such as Chapter 1 teachers) with those of regular classroom teachers. This integration was done differently in the two evaluations of the full CIRC program. In the 12-week pilot study (Madden, Stevens, and Slavin 1986b), resource and remedial reading teachers removed students from their reading classes for part or all of the reading period and implemented the CIRC program in separate areas. However, in a 24-week full-scale evaluation (Stevens et al. 1987; Madden, Stevens, and Slavin 1986b), the schools scheduled resource and remedial reading pullouts at times other than reading or language arts/writing periods. Special and remedial reading teachers attended the CIRC training sessions but did not use CIRC methods or materials in their pullout programs, except that they occasionally helped students with problems they were encountering in the CIRC program used in the regular class.

As of this writing, two studies have evaluated the impact of the full CIRC program. The first study (Madden, Stevens, and Slavin 1986b; Stevens et al. 1987) evaluated the full CIRC program over a 12-week period. Overall, the effects of the CIRC program on student achievement were quite positive. CIRC classes gained 30 to 36 percent of a grade equivalent more than control students in reading comprehension and reading vocabulary, 52 percent of a grade equivalent more in language expression, 25 percent of a grade equivalent more in language mechanics, and 72 percent of a grade equivalent more in spelling. On writing samples, CIRC students outperformed control students on ratings of organization, ideas, and mechanics. The effects of CIRC were equal for students at all levels of prior achievement: high, average, and low.

The second study (Stevens et al. 1987) was designed to evaluate the CIRC program in third and fourth grade classes over a full school year, incorporating changes suggested by the pilot study. For the total samples involved, the results of Study 2 were even more positive than those of Study 1. On the reading comprehension, language expression, and language mechanics scales of the California Achievement Test, CIRC students gained significantly more than control students, averaging gains of almost two-thirds of a grade equivalent more than control students. Differences of 20 percent of a grade equivalent on reading vocabulary were not significant, however. On writing samples, CIRC students again outperformed control students on organization, ideas, and mechanics ratings.

Study 2 added informal reading inventories as measures of students' oral reading skills. CIRC students scored significantly higher than control students on word recognition, word analysis, fluency, error rate, and grade placement measures of the Durrell Informal Reading Inventory, with effect sizes ranging from 44 percent to 64 percent of a standard deviation. As in Study 1, the CIRC program produced equal gains for students initially high, average, and low in reading skills, although mainstreamed academically handicapped students made particularly impressive gains (Slavin, Stevens, and Madden 1988).

A PRIMARY INSTRUCTIONAL METHOD

Research on TAI and CIRC has clearly supported the idea that complex, comprehensive approaches that combine cooperative learning with other instructional elements can be effective in increasing the achievement of all students in heterogeneous classes. Studies demonstrate that cooperative learning programs can be used as the primary instructional method in reading, writing, and mathematics—not just as an additional strategy to add to teachers' repertoires.

One important possibility opened up by the development of TAI and

116

CIRC is the use of cooperative learning as the unifying element of school reform. Cooperative learning methods are critical elements of the cooperative school (Slavin 1987b), a school-level change model that incorporates widespread use of cooperative learning, peer coaching, comprehensive mainstreaming, and teacher involvement in decision making.

Comprehensive cooperative learning models can also serve as a vehicle for introducing developments from the fields of curriculum and educational psychology into routine classroom use. Cooperative learning provides a structure for incorporating identification of story elements, prediction, summarization, direct instruction in reading comprehension, and integration of reading and writing within the reading period. It provides a structure that can enhance the effectiveness and practicality of writing process methods or of adapting instruction to individual needs in mathematics. Thus cooperative learning is not only an innovation in itself but also a catalyst for other needed changes in curriculum and instruction.

If educational methods are to effect major changes in student achievement, they must address many elements of classroom organization and instruction at the same time. TAI and CIRC are two examples of what the future may hold in applying the best knowledge we have to improving instruction methodology.

Author's note: Preparation of this article was supported by a grant from the Office of Educational Research and Improvement, U.S. Department of Education (No. OERI-G-86-0006). However, any opinions expressed are ours, and do not represent Department of Education policy.

---

[1]TAI is currently published under the title "Team Accelerated Instruction" by Charlesbridge Publishing, 85 Main St., Watertown, MA 02171.
[2]We use *significant* in the sense of *statistically significant* throughout this paper.

REFERENCES

Allan, S. "Ability-Grouping Research Reviews: What Do They Say About the Gifted?" *Educational Leadership* 48, no. 6 1991: 60-65.

Allen, W.H., and VanSickle, R.L.. "Learning Teams and Low Achievers." *Social Education* (1984): 60-64.

Allport, G. *The Nature of Prejudice.* Cambridge, Mass.: Addison-Wesley, 1954.

Aronson, E.; Blaney, N.; Stephan, C.; Sikes, J.; and Snapp, M. 1978. *The Jigsaw Classroom.* Beverly Hills, Calif.: Sage, 1978.

Ballard, M.; Corman, L.; Gottlieb, J.; and Kaufman, M. "Improving the Social Status of Mainstreamed Retarded Children." *Journal of Educational Psychology* 69 (1977): 605-11.

Blaney, N. T.; Stephan, S.; Rosenfeld, D.; Aronson, E.; and Sikes, J. "Interdependence in the Classroom: A Field Study." *Journal of Educational Psychology* 69, no. 2 (1977): 121-28.

Bossert, S.T. "Cooperative Activities in the Classroom." In *Review of Research in Education,* edited by E.Z. Rothkopf, vol. 15. Washington, D.C.: American Educational Research Association, 1988–89.

Bronfenbrenner, U. *Two Worlds of Childhood.* New York: Russell Sage Foundation, 1970.

Coleman, J.S. *The Adolescent Society.* New York: Free Press of Glencoe, 1961.

Cooper, L.; Johnson, D.W.; Johnson, R.; and Wilderson, F. "Effects of Cooperative, Competitive, and Individualistic Experiences on Interpersonal Attraction among Heterogeneous Peers." *Journal of Social Psychology* 111 (1980): 243-52.

Dansereau, D.F. "Cooperative Learning Strategies." In *Learning and Study Strategies: Issues in Assessment, Instruction, and Evaluation,* edited by E.E. Weinstein, E.T. Goetz, and P.A. Alexander. New York: Academic Press, 1988.

Davidson, N. "Small-Group Learning and Teaching in Mathematics: A Selective Review of the Research." In *Learning to Cooperate, Cooperating to Learn,* edited by R.E. Slavin, S. Sharan, S. Kagan, R. Hertz-Lazarowitz, C. Webb, and R. Schmuck. New York: Plenum, 1985.

Deutsch, M. "A Theory of Cooperation and Competition." *Human Relations* 2 (1949): 129-52.

DeVries, D.L.; Edwards, K.J.; and Slavin, R.E. "Biracial Learning Teams and Race Relations in the Classroom: Four Field Experiments on Teams-Games-Tournament." *Journal of Educational Psychology* 70 (1978): 356-62.

DeVries, D.L.; Lucasse, P.; and Shackman, S. "Small-Group Versus Individualized Instruction: A Field Test of Their Relative Effectiveness." Paper presented at the annual convention of the American Psychological Association, New York, 1979.

DeVries, D.L., and Slavin, R.E. "Teams-Games-Tournament (TGT): Review of Ten Classroom Experiments." *Journal of Research and Development in Education* 12 1978: 28-38.

Fox, L.H. "Programs for the Gifted and Talented: An Overview." In *The Gifted and Talented: Their Education and Development,* edited by A.H. Passow. Chicago: University of Chicago Press, 1979.

Fraser, S.C.; Beaman, A.L.; Diener, E.; and R.T. Kelem, "Two, Three, or Four Heads Are Better Than One: Modification of College Performance by Peer Monitoring." *Journal of Educational Psychology* 69, no. 2 (1977): 101-8.

Gerard, H.B., and Miller, N. *School Desegregation: A Long-Range Study.* New York: Plenum Press, 1975.

Gickling, E., and Theobold, J. "Mainstreaming: Affect or Effect." *Journal of Special Education* 9 (1975): 317-28.

Gonzales, A. "Classroom Cooperation and Ethnic Balance." Paper presented at the annual convention of the American Psychological Association, New York, 1979.

Good, T., and Grouws, D. "The Missouri Mathematics Effectiveness Project: An Experimental Study in Fourth Grade Classrooms." *Journal of Educational Psychology* 71 (1979): 355-62.

Gottlieb, J., and Leyser, Y. "Friendship between Mentally Retarded and Nonretarded Children." In *The Development of Children's Friendships,* edited by S. Asher and J. Gottman. Cambridge: Cambridge University Press, 1981.

Graves, D. *Writing: Teachers and Children at Work.* Exeter, N.H.: Heinemann, 1983.

Hartley, W. *Prevention Outcomes of Small-Group Education with School Children: An Epidemiologic Follow-Up of the Kansas City School Behavior Project.* Kansas City: University of Kansas Medical Center, 1976.

Horak, V.M. "A Meta-Analysis of Research Findings on Individualized Instruction in Mathematics." *Journal of Educational Research* 74 (1981): 249-53.

Howell, W. "Grouping of Talented Students Leads to Better Academic Achievement in Secondary School." *Bulletin of the NASSP* 46 (1962): 67-73.

Humphreys, B.; Johnson, R.; and Johnson, D.W. "Effects of Cooperative, Competitive, and Individualistic Learning on Students' Achievements in Science Class." *Journal of Research in Science Teaching* 19 (1982): 351-56.

Janke, R. "The Teams-Games-Tournament (TGT) Method and the Behavioral Adjustment and Academic Achievement of Emotionally Impaired Adolescents." Paper presented at the annual convention of the American Educational Research Association, Toronto, April 1978.

Johnson, D.W., and Johnson, R.T. *Learning Together and Alone.* 2nd ed. Englewood, N.J.: Prentice-Hall, 1987.

Johnson, D.W., and Johnson, R.T. "Toward a Cooperative Effort: A Response to Slavin." *Educational Leadership* 46, no. 2 (1989): 80-81.

Johnson, D.W., Johnson, R.T.; and Maruyama, G. "Interdependence and Interpersonal Attraction among Heterogeneous and Homogeneous Individuals: A Theoretical Formulation and a Meta-Analysis of the Research." *Review of Educational Research* 53 (1983): 5-54.

Johnson, D.W., Maruyama, G.; Johnson, R.; Nelson, D.; and Skon, L. "Effects of Cooperative, Competitive, and Individualistic Goal Structures on Achievement: A Meta-Analysis." *Psychological Bulletin* 89 (1981): 47-62.

Kulik, C.-L., and Kulik, J.A. "Effects of Ability Grouping on Secondary School Students: A Meta-Analysis of Evaluation Findings." *American Educational Research Journal* 9 (1982): 415-28.

___. "Effects of Ability Grouping on Student Achievement." *Equity and Excellence* 23 (1987): 22-30.

Kulik, J.A., and Kulik, C.-L. "Effects of Accelerated Instruction on Students." *Review of Educational Research* 54 (1984): 409-25.

Madden, N.A., and Slavin, R.E. "Cooperative Learning and Social Acceptance of Mainstreamed Academically Handicapped Students." *Journal of Special Education* 17 (1983a): 171-82.

____. "Mainstreaming Students with Mild Academic Handicaps: Academic and Social Outcomes. *Review of Educational Research* 53 (1983b): 519-69.

Madden, N.A.; Farnish, A.M.; Slavin, R.E.; and Stevens, R.J. *Cooperative Integrated Reading and Composition: Teacher's Manual for Writing.* Baltimore, Md: Center for Research on Elementary and Middle Schools, Johns Hopkins University, 1986.

Madden, N.A.; Stevens, R.J.; and Slavin, R.E. *A Comprehensive Cooperative Learning Approach to Elementary Reading and Writing: Effects on Student Achievement.* Report No. 2. Baltimore, Md: Center for Research on Elementary and Middle Schools, Johns Hopkins University, 1986a.

____. *Reading Instruction in the Mainstream: A Cooperative Learning Approach.* Technical Report No. 5. Baltimore, Md: Center for Research on Elementary and Middle Schools, Johns Hopkins University, 1986b.

Madden, N.A.; Stevens, R.J.; Slavin, R.E.; and Farnish, A.M. *Cooperative Integrated Reading and Composition: Teacher's Manual for Reading.* Baltimore, Md.: Center for Research on Elementary and Middle Schools, Johns Hopkins University, 1988.

Mattingly, R.M.; and VanSickle, R.L. *Jigsaw II in Secondary Social Studies: An Experiment.* Athens, Ga.: University of Georgia, 1990.

Mikkelson, J.E. "An Experimental Study of Selective Grouping and Acceleration in Junior High School Mathematics." Ph.D. diss., University of Minnesota, 1962.

Miller, R.L. "Individualized Instruction in Mathematics: A Review of Research." *Mathematics Teacher* 69 (1976): 345-51.

Moskowitz, J.M.; Malvin, J.H.; Schaeffer, G.A.; and Schaps, E. "Evaluation of a Cooperative Learning Strategy." *American Educational Research Journal* 20 (1983): 687-96.

Newman, F.M., and Thompson, J. *Effects of Cooperative Learning on Achievement in Secondary Schools: A Summary of Research.* Madison: University of Wisconsin, National Center on Effective Secondary Schools, 1987.

Oishi, S. " Effects of Team-Assisted Individualization in Mathematics on Cross-Race Interactions of Elementary School Children." Ph.D. diss., University of Maryland, 1983.

Okebukola, P.A. "The Relative Effectiveness of Cooperative and Competitive Interaction Techniques in Strengthening Students' Performance in Science Classes." *Science Education* 69 (1985): 501-9.

Sharan, S.; Hertz-Lazarowitz, R.; and Ackerman, Z. "Academic Achievement of Elementary School Children in Small-Group vs. Whole-Class Instruction." *Journal of Experimental Education* 48 (1980): 125-29.

Sharan, S.; Kussell, P.; Hertz-Lazarowitz, R.; Bejarano, Y.; Raviv, S.; and Sharan, Y. *Cooperative Learning in the Classroom: Research in Desegregated Schools.* Hillsdale, N.J.: Erlbaum, 1984.

Sharan, S., and Shachar, C. *Language and Learning in the Cooperative Classroom.* New York: Springer, 1988.

Sharan, S., and Sharan, Y. *Small-Group Teaching.* Englewood, N.J.: Educational Technology Publications, 1976.

Sherman, L.W., and Thomas, M. "Mathematics Achievement in Cooperative Versus Individualistic Goal-Structured High School Classrooms." *Journal of Educational Research* 79 (1986): 169-72.

Slavin, R.E. "Classroom Reward Structure: An Analytic and Practical Review." *Review of Educational Research* 47, no. 4 (1977a): 633-50.

____. *Student Learning Team Techniques: Narrowing the Achievement Gap between the Races.* Report No. 228. Baltimore, Md.: Center for Social Organization of Schools, Johns Hopkins University, 1977b.

____. "A Student Team Approach to Teaching Adolescents with Special Emotional and Behavioral Needs." *Psychology in the Schools* 14, no. 1 (1977c): 77-84.

____. "Student Teams and Achievement Divisions." *Journal of Research and Development in Education* 12 (1978): 39-49.

____. "Effects of Biracial Learning Teams on Cross-Racial Friendships." *Journal of Educational Psychology* 71 (1979): 381-87.

____. "Effects of Individual Learning Expectations on Student Achievement." *Journal of Educational Psychology* 72 (1980): 520-24.

____. *Cooperative Learning.* New York: Longman, 1983a.

____. "When Does Cooperative Learning Increase Student Achievement?" *Psychological Bulletin* 94 (1983b): 429-45.

____. "Meta-Analysis in Education: How Has It Been Used?" *Educational Researcher* 13, no. 8 (1984): 6-15, 24-27.

____. "Cooperative Learning: Applying Contact Theory in Desegregated Schools." *Journal of Social Issues* 41, no. 3 (1985a): 45-62.

____. "Team-Assisted Individualization: Combining Cooperative Learning and Individualized Instruction in Mathematics." In *Learning to Cooperate, Cooperating to Learn,* edited by R.E. Slavin, S. Sharan, S. Kagan, R. Hertz-Lazarowitz, C. Webb, and R. Schmuck. New York: Plenum, 1985b.

____. "Team-Assisted Individualization: A Cooperative Learning Solution for Adaptive Instruction in Mathematics." In *Adapting Instruction to Individual Differences,* edited by M. Wang and H. Walberg, pp. 236-53. Berkeley, Calif.: McCutchan, 1985c.

____. *Using Student Team Learning.* 3d ed. Baltimore, Md: Center for Research on Elementary and Middle Schools, Johns Hopkins University, 1986.

____. "Ability Grouping and Student Achievement in Elementary Schools: A Best Evidence Synthesis." *Review of Educational Research* 57 (1987a): 213-336.

____. "Cooperative Learning and the Cooperative School." *Educational Leadership* 45, no. 3 (1987b): 7-13.

____. *Cooperative Learning: Student Teams.* 2d ed. Washington, D.C.: National Education Association, 1987c.

____. "Cooperative Learning and Student Achievement." *Educational Leadership* 45, no. 2 (1988a): 31-33.

____. "Synthesis of Research on Grouping in Elementary and Secondary Schools." *Educational Leadership* 46, no. 1 (1988b): 66-77.

___. "Cooperative Learning and Student Achievement." In *School and Classroom Organization,* edited by R.E. Slavin. Hillsdale, N.J.: Erlbaum, (1989a).

___. "Slavin Replies." *Educational Leadership* 46, no. 7 (1989b): 81.

___. "Ability Grouping, Cooperative Learning, and the Gifted." *Journal for the Education of the Gifted* 14 (1990a): 3-8.

___. "Achievement Effects of Ability Grouping in Secondary Schools: A Best-Evidence Synthesis." *Review of Educational Research* 60, no. 3 (1990b): 471-99.

___. *Cooperative Learning: Theory, Research, and Practice.* Englewood Cliffs, N.J.: Prentice-Hall, 1990c.

Slavin, R.E.; Braddock, J.H.; Hall, C.; and Petza, R.J. *Alternatives to Ability Grouping.* Center for Research on Effective Schooling for Disadvantaged Students, Johns Hopkins University, 1989.

Slavin, R.E.; and Karweit, N. "Cognitive and Affective Outcomes of an Intensive Student Team Learning Experience." *Journal of Experimental Education* 50 (1981): 29-35.

___. "Mastery Learning and Student Teams: A Factorial Experiment in Urban General Mathematics Classes." *American Educational Research Journal* 21 (1984): 725-36.

Slavin, R.E., and Karweit, N.L. "Effects of Whole-Class, Ability-Grouped, and Individualized Instruction on Mathematics Achievement." *American Educational Research Journal* 22 (1985): 351-67.

Slavin, R.E.; Leavey, M.; and Madden, N.A. "Effects of Student Teams and Individualized Instruction on Student Mathematics Achievement, Attitudes, and Behaviors." Paper presented at the annual convention of the American Educational Research Association, New York, 1982.

___. "Combining Cooperative Learning and Individualized Instruction: Effects on Student Mathematics Achievement Attitudes and Behaviors." *Elementary School Journal* 84 (1984): 409-22.

Slavin, R.E.; Leavey, M.B.; and Madden, N.A. *Team Accelerated Instruction—Mathematics.* Watertown, Mass.: Mastery Education Corporation, 1986.

Slavin, R.E.; Madden, N.A.; and Leavey, M.B. "Effects of Team-Assisted Individualization on the Mathematics Achievement of Academically Handicapped and Nonhandicapped Students." *Journal of Educational Psychology* 76 (1984): 813-19.

Slavin, R.E., and E. Oickle, "Effects of Cooperative Learning Teams on Student Achievement and Race Relations: Treatment by Race Interactions." *Sociology of Education* 54 (1981): 174-80.

Slavin, R.E.; Stevens, R.J.; and Madden, N.A. "Accommodating Student Diversity in Reading and Writing Instruction: A Cooperative Learning Approach." *Remedial and Special Education* 9, no. 1 (1988): 60-66.

Smith, K.A.; Johnson, D.W.; and Johnson, R.T. "Can Conflict Be Constructive? Controversy Versus Concurrence Seeking in Learning Groups." *Journal of Educational Psychology* 73 (1981): 651-63.

Solomon, D.; Watson, M.; Schaps, E.; Battistich, V.; and Solomon, J. "Cooperative Learning as Part of a Comprehensive Classroom Program Designed to Promote Prosocial Development." In *Current Research on Cooperative Learning,* edited by S. Sharan. New York: Praeger, 1990.

Stevens, R.J.; Madden, N.A.; Slavin, R.E.; and Farnish, A.M. " Cooperative Integrated

Reading and Composition: Two Field Experiments." *Reading Research Quarterly* 22 (1987): 433-54.

Stevens, R.J.; Slavin, R.E.; and Farnish, A.M. "A Cooperative Learning Approach to Elementary Reading and Writing Instruction: Long-Term Effects." Paper presented at the annual convention of the American Educational Research Association, Boston, April 1990.

Stevens, R.J.; Slavin, R.E.; Farnish, A.M.; and Madden, N.A. "The Effects of Cooperative Learning and Direct Instruction in Reading Comprehension Strategies on Main Idea Identification." Paper presented at the annual convention of the American Educational Research Association,New Orleans, La, April 1988.

Webb, N. "Student Interaction and Learning in Small Groups: A Research Summary." In *Learning to Cooperate, Cooperating to Learn,* edited by R. Slavin, S. Sharan, S. Kagan, R. Hertz-Lazarowitz, C. Webb, and R. Schmuck. New York: Plenum, 1985.

Wiatrowski, M.; Hansell, S.; Massey, C.R.; and Wilson, D.L. "Curriculum Tracking and Delinquency." *American Sociological Review* 47 (1982): 151-60.

Willis, S. "Cooperative Learning Fallout." *ASCD Update* 32, no. 8 (1990): 6, 8.

Yager, S.; Johnson, D.W.; and Johnson, R.T. "Oral Discussion, Group-to-Individual Transfer, and Achievement in Cooperative Learning Groups." *Journal of Educational Psychology* 77 (1985): 60-66.

Ziegler, S. "The Effectiveness of Cooperative Learning Teams for Increasing Cross-Ethnic Friendship: Additional Evidence." *Human Organization* 40 (1981): 264-68.

SELECTED ADDITIONAL RESOURCES

Austin, J.R. "Competition: Is Music Education the Loser?" *Music Educators Journal* 76, no. 6 (1990): 21-25.

Behounek, K.J., et al. "Our Class Has Twenty-Five Teachers." *Arithmetic Teacher* 36, no. 4 (1988): 10-13.

Brandt, R. "On Cooperation in Schools: A Conversation with David and Roger Johnson." *Educational Leadership* 45, no. 3 (1987): 14-19.

Bregman, G. "Cooperative Learning: A New Strategy for the Artroom." *School Arts* 89, no. 2 (1989): 32-33.

Bump, E. "Utilizing Cooperative Learning to Teach Social Studies in the Middle School." *Social Science Record* 26, no. 4 (1989): 32-36.

Casella, V. "Peer Pressure Turns into Peer Cooperation in This Computer Classroom." *Instructor* 98, no. 6 (1989): 34.

Clemson, R., and McTighe, J. "Teaching Teachers to Make Connections: A Challenge for Teacher Educators." *Action in Teacher Education* 12, no. 1 (1990): 55-60.

Cohen, E. *Designing Groupwork.* New York: Teachers College Press, Columbia University, 1986.

Dalton, D.W. "The Effects of Cooperative Learning Strategies on Achievement and Attitudes during Interactive Video." *Journal of Computer-Based Instruction* 17, no. 1 (1990): 8-16.

Dansereau, D.F. "Learning Strategy Research." In *Thinking and Learning Skills: Relating Instruction to Basic Research,* edited by J. Segal, S. Chipman, and R. Glaser. Hillsdale, N.J.: Erlbaum, 1985.

Davidson, N., and O'Leary, P.W. "How Cooperative Learning Can Enhance Mastery Teaching." *Educational Leadership* 47, no. 5 (1990): 30-33.

DeVillar, R.A. "Computers, Software, and Cooperative Learning: Effective Peer Communication in the Heterogeneous Classroom." *Teacher Education Quarterly* 16, no. 2 (1989): 91-95.

DeZure, D. "Matching Classroom Structure to Narrative Technique: Using 'Jigsawing' to Teach 'Ordinary People,' A Multiperspective Novel." *CEA Forum* 19, no. 3–4 (1989): 17-20.

Dishon, D., and O'Leary, P.W. *A Guidebook for Cooperative Learning.* Portage, Mich.: Cooperation Unlimited, 1984.

Dunn, R.E., and Goldman, M. "Competition and Noncompetition in Relationship to Satisfaction and Feelings Toward Own-Group and Nongroup Members." *Journal of Social Psychology* 68 (1966): 299-311.

Ferguson, P. "Cooperative Team Learning: Theory into Practice for the Prospective Middle School Teacher," *Action in Teacher Education* 11, no. 4 (1990): 24-28.

Goldberg, M.F. "A Portrait of Two Writing Teachers. *Educational Leadership* 47, no. 6 (1990): 70-71.

Gollert, H., et al. "A Touch of. . .Class." *Canadian Modern Language Review* 45, no. 4 (1989): 715-23.

Hall, R.H., et al. "The Role of Individual Differences in the Cooperative Learning of Technical Material." *Journal of Educational Psychology* 80, no. 2 (1988): 172-78.

Johnson, D.W., and Johnson, R.T. "Instructional Goal Structure: Cooperative, Competitive, or Individualistic." *Review of Educational Research* 44 (1974): 213-40.

___. "Effects of Cooperative and Individualistic Learning Experiences on Interethnic Interaction." *Journal of Educational Psychology* 73 (1981): 444-49.

___. "Social Skills for Successful Group Work." *Educational Leadership* 47, no. 4 (1990): 29-33.

Johnson, D.W.; Johnson, R.T.; Holubec, E.J.; and Roy, P. *Circles of Learning*. Alexandria, Va.: Association for Supervision and Curriculum Development, 1986.

Johnson, D.W., et al. "Different Cooperative Learning Procedures and Cross-Handicap Relationships." *Exceptional Children* 53, no. 3 (1986): 247-52.

___. "Impact of Goal and Resource Interdependence on Problem-Solving Success." *Journal of Social Psychology* 129, no. 5 (1989): 621-29.

Johnson, R.T., and Johnson, D.W. "Action Research: Cooperative Learning in the Science Classroom." *Science and Children* 24, no. 2 (1986): 31-32.

___. "How Can We Put Cooperative Learning into Practice?" *Science Teacher* 54, no. 6 (1987): 46-48.

Johnson, R.T., et al. "Comparison of Computer-Assisted Cooperative, Competitive, and Individualistic Learning." *American Educational Research Journal* 23, no. 3 (1986): 382-92.

Jones, R.M., and Steinbrink, J.E. "Using Cooperative Groups in Science Teaching." *School Science and Mathematics* 89, no. 7 (1989): 541-51.

Jones, S.C., and Vroom, V.H. "Division of Labor and Performance under Cooperative and Competitive Conditions." *Journal of Abnormal and Social Psychology* 68 (1964): 313-20.

Kagan, S. *Cooperative Learning Resources for Teachers*. San Juan Capistrano, Calif.: Resources for Teachers, 1989.

Long, G.A. "Cooperative Learning: A New Approach." *Journal of Agricultural Education* 30, no. 2 (1989): 2-9.

Lott, A.F., and Lott, B.E. "Group Cohesiveness as Interpersonal Attraction: A Review of Relationships with Antecedent and Consequent Variables." *Psychological Bulletin* 64 (1965): 259-309.

Lourie, N.E. "How Do You Get There from Here? Implementing Cooperative Learning in the Classroom." *Social Studies Review* 28, no. 3 (1989): 18-25.

Lyman, L., and Foyle, H.C. "The Constitution in Action: A Cooperative Learning Approach." *Georgia Social Science Journal* 21, no. 1 (1990): 24-34.

McGroarty, M. "The Benefits of Cooperative Learning Arrangements in Second Language Instruction." *NABE: The Journal for the National Association for Bilingual Education* 13, no. 2 (1989): 127-43.

Madden, L. "Cooperative Learning Strategies in Elementary School." *Illinois School Research and Development* 24, no. 2 (1988): 41-46.

___. "Improve Reading Attitudes of Poor Readers Through Cooperative Reading Teams." *Reading Teacher* 42, no. 3 (1988): 194-99.

Manera, E.S., and Glockhamer, H. "Cooperative Learning: Do Students 'Own' the Content?" *Action in Teacher Education* 10, no. 4 (1989): 53-56.

Margolis, H., et al. "Using Cooperative Learning to Facilitate Mainstreaming in the Social Studies." *Social Education* 54, no. 2 (1990): 111-14.

Martens, M.L. "Getting a Grip on Groups." *Science and Children* 27, no. 5 (1990): 18-19.

Miller, D.E. "Cooperative Critical Thinking and History." *Social Studies Review* 28, no. 3 (1989): 55-68.

Miller, K.A. "Enhancing Early Childhood Mainstreaming Through Cooperative Learning: A Brief Literature Review." *Child Study Journal* 19, no. 4 (1989): 285-92.

Myers, J., and Lemon, C. "The Jigsaw Strategy: Cooperative Learning in Social Studies." *History and Social Science Teacher* 24, no. 1 (1988): 18-22.

Nattiv, A., et al. "Conflict Resolution and Interpersonal Skill Building Through the Use of Cooperative Learning." *Journal of Humanistic Education and Development* 28, no. 2 (1989): 96-103.

O'Donnell, A.M., et al. "Promoting Functional Literacy Through Cooperative Learning." *Journal of Reading Behavior* 20, no. 4 (1988): 339-56.

Onslow, B. "Pentominoes Revisited." *Arithmetic Teacher* 37, no. 9 (1990): 5-9.

Peck, G. "Facilitating Cooperative Learning: A Forgotten Tool Gets It Started." *Academic Therapy* 25, no. 2 (1989): 145-50.

Perry, T.L. "Cooperative Learning = Effective Therapy." *Language, Speech, and Hearing Services in Schools* 21, no. 2 (1990): 120.

Prescott, S. "Teachers' Perceptions of Factors That Affect Successful Implementation of Cooperative Learning." *Action in Teacher Education* 11, no. 4 (1990): 30-34.

Reynolds, C., and Salend, S.J. "Cooperative Learning in Special Education Teacher Preparation Programs." *Teacher Education and Special Education* 12, no. 3 (1989): 91-95.

Rich, Y. "Ideological Impediments to Instructional Innovation: The Case of Cooperative Learning." *Teaching and Teacher Education* 6, no. 1 (1990): 81-91.

Rosenbaum, L., et al. "Step into Problem Solving with Cooperative Learning." *Arithmetic Teacher* 36, no. 7 (1989): 7-11.

Ross, J.A. "Improving Social-Environmental Studies Problem Solving Through Cooperative Learning. *American Educational Research Journal* 25, no. 4 (1988): 573-91.

Ross, J.A., and Raphael, D. "Communication and Problem-Solving Achievement in Cooperative Learning Groups." *Journal of Curriculum Studies* 22, no. 2 (1990): 149-64.

Sabato, G. "Cooperation and Competition Unleash Creative Potential." *Social Studies Review* 28, no. 3 (1989): 103-9.

Salend, S.J., and Sonnenschein, P. "Validating the Effectiveness of a Cooperative Learning Strategy Through Direct Observation." *Journal of School Psychology* 27, no. 1 (1989): 47-58.

Salend, S.J., and Washin, B. "Team-Assisted Individualization with Handicapped Adjudicated Youth." *Exceptional Children* 55, no. 2 (1988): 174-80.

Sharan, S., and Shachar, C. "Cooperative Learning Effects on Students' Academic Achievement and Verbal Behavior in Multiethnic Junior High School Classrooms in Israel." University of Tel Aviv, Israel. Unpublished paper, 1986.

Slavin, R.E. "Students Motivating Students to Excel: Cooperative Incentives, Cooperative Tasks, and Student Achievement." *Elementary School Journal* 85, no. 1 (1984): 53-63.

___. "Team-Assisted Individualization: Cooperative Learning and Individualized Instruction in the Mainstreamed Classroom." *Remedial and Special Education* 5, no. 6 (1984): 33-42.

___. *Educational Psychology: Theory into Practice.* Englewood Cliffs, N.J.: Prentice-Hall, 1986.

___. "Combining Cooperative Learning and Individualized Instruction." *Arithmetic Teacher* 35, no. 3 (1987): 14-16.

___. "Cooperative Learning: Where Behavioral and Humanistic Approaches to Classroom Motivation Meet." *Elementary School Journal* 88, no. 1 (1987): 29-37.

___. "Developmental and Motivational Perspectives on Cooperative Learning: A Reconciliation," *Child Development* 58, no. 5 (1987): 1161-67.

___. "Comprehensive Cooperative Learning Models for Heterogeneous Classrooms." *Pointer* 33, no. 2 (1989): 12-19.

___. "Research on Cooperative Learning: An International Perspective." *Scandinavian Journal of Educational Research* 33, no. 4 (1989): 231-43.

___. "Are Cooperative Learning and 'Untracking' Harmful to the Gifted?" *Educational Leadership* 48, no. 6 (1991): 68-71.

Slavin, R.E.; Sharan, S.; Kagan, S.; Hertz-Lazarowitz, R.; Webb, C.; and R. Schmuck, eds. *Learning to Cooperate, Cooperating to Learn.* New York: Plenum, 1985.

Smith, C.B. "Shared Learning Promotes Critical Reading (ERIC/RCS)." *Reading Teacher* 43, no. 1 (1989): 76-77.

Stiers, D. "Cooperative Learning for Remedial Students." *Social Studies Review* 28, no. 3 (1989): 46-48.

Taymans, J.M. "Cooperative Learning for Learning-Disabled Adolescents." *Pointer* 33, no. 2 (1989): 28-32.

Thomas, E.J. "Effects of Facilitative Role Interdependence on Group Functioning." *Human Relations* 10 (1957): 347-66.

Topping, K. "Peer Tutoring and Paired Reading: Combining Two Powerful Techniques." *Reading Teacher* 42, no. 7 (1989): 488-94.

Uttero, D.A. "Activating Comprehension Through Cooperative Learning." *Reading Teacher* 41, no. 4 (1988): 390-95.

Van Cleaf, D.W. "Cooperative Learning: Linking Reading and Social Studies." *Reading Psychology* 9, no. 1 (1988): 59-63.

Watson, D.L., and Rangel, L. "Don't Forget the Slow Learner." *Clearing House* 62, no. 6 (1989): 66-68.

Watson, M.S., et al. "Cooperative Learning as a Means of Promoting Prosocial Development among Kindergarten and Early Primary-Grade Children." *International Journal of Social Education* 3, no. 2 (1988): 34-47.

Weigel, R.H.; Wiser, P.L.; and Cook, S.W. "Impact of Cooperative Learning Experiences on Cross-Ethnic Relations and Attitudes." *Journal of Social Issues* 31, no. 1 (1975): 219-45.